This was purchased with funds generously donated by the Mirant Corporation!

WITHDRAWN

AnimalWays

Whales

AnimalWays

Whales

Dan Greenberg

BENCHMARK BOOKS

MARSHALL CAVENDISH
NEW YORK

With thanks to Paul Sieswerda of the New York Aquarium for his expert reading of this manuscript.

Benchmark Books
Marshall Cavendish
99 White Plains Road
Tarrytown, NY 10591-9001
www.marshallcavendish.com

Library of Congress Cataloging-in-Publication Data
Greenberg, Daniel A.
Whales / by Dan Greenberg
p. cm. — (Animal ways)
Summary: Describes in detail the physical characteristics, behavior, migration and life cycle of various kinds of whales, among the largest creatures ever known to have lived on Earth, and discusses the history of human interaction with these animals.
Includes bibliographical references and index (p. 110)
ISBN 0-7614-1389-8
1. Whales—Juvenile literature. [1. Whales.] I. Title. II. Series
QL737.C4 G739   2002   599.5—dc21   2001043883

Photo Research by Candlepants Incorporated

Cover Photo: Animals Animals/James Watt

The photographs in this book are used by permission and through the courtesy of: *Animals Animals*: Gerard Lacz, 2, 32, 33, 44, 93; James Watt, 12, 21, 43; G.L. Kooyman, 25; Joe McDonald, 31; Michael F. Sacca, 37; Phyllis Greenberg, 47; Bob Cranston, 67, 97; Shane Moore, 69; Richard Kolar, 70; Bradley W. Stahl, 72; Will Darnell, 88; Richard Sobol, 91; Mark Stouffer, 95; Doug Wechsler, 98; Stefano Nicolini, 101; *Photo Researchers Inc.* : Francois Gohier, 9, 22, 51, 55, 65, 73, 77, 80, 103; Tom McHugh, 52, 58; William H. Mullins, 57; Hubbertus Kanus, 63; Gregory Ochocki, 75; Stewart Westmorland, 79, 85; *Corbis*: Hulton Deutsch Collection, 11; Bettmann, 19; *Art Resource, NY*: Giradon, 14; Image Select, 17; *Marine Mammal Images*: James Watt, 34, 74; Michael Nolan, 41; ACS-G.Bakker, 46; Mark Conlin, 54; Alicia Shulman, 104; *New Bedford Whaling Museum*: back cover.

Printed in Italy

6 5 4 3 2 1

Contents

Animal Kingdom

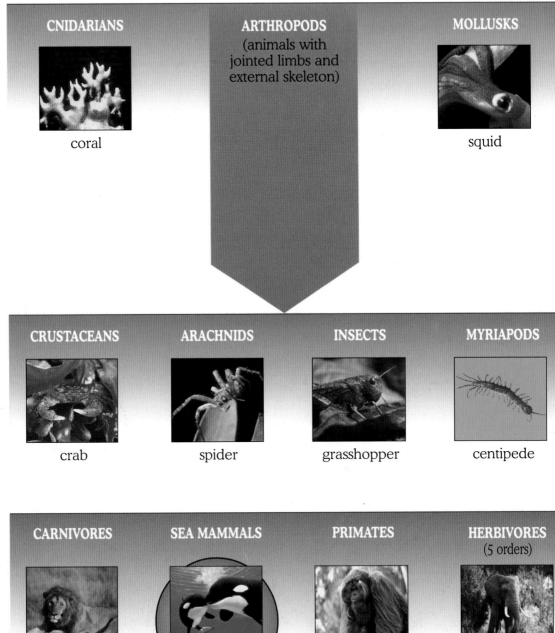

CNIDARIANS

coral

ARTHROPODS
(animals with
jointed limbs and
external skeleton)

MOLLUSKS

squid

CRUSTACEANS

crab

ARACHNIDS

spider

INSECTS

grasshopper

MYRIAPODS

centipede

CARNIVORES

lion

SEA MAMMALS

WHALE

PRIMATES

orangutan

HERBIVORES
(5 orders)

elephant

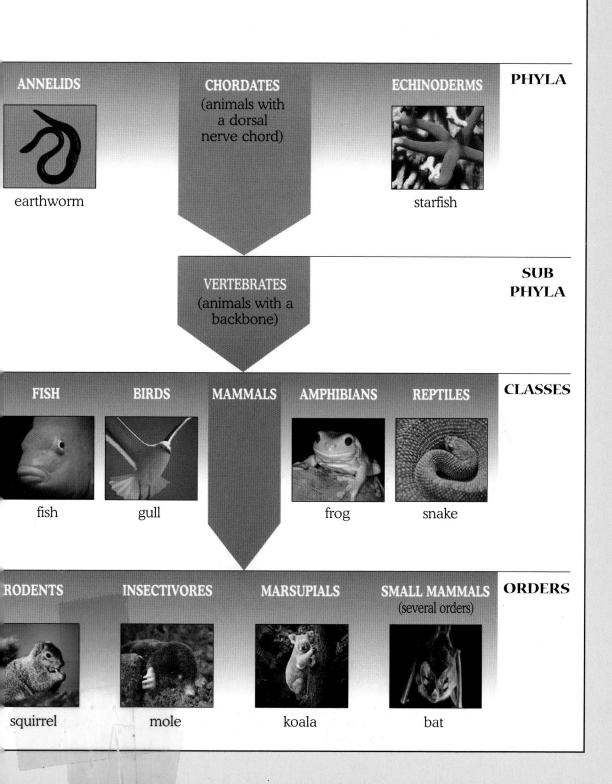

PHYLA

ANNELIDS

earthworm

CHORDATES
(animals with
a dorsal
nerve chord)

ECHINODERMS

starfish

**SUB
PHYLA**

VERTEBRATES
(animals with a
backbone)

CLASSES

FISH

fish

BIRDS

gull

MAMMALS

AMPHIBIANS

frog

REPTILES

snake

ORDERS

RODENTS

squirrel

INSECTIVORES

mole

MARSUPIALS

koala

SMALL MAMMALS
(several orders)

bat

1   Amazing Whales

The boat, a whale-watching vessel, is now about 20 miles (30 km) off the New England shore. It is quiet. The water is calm; the sky is a clear pale blue. And then, off to the right, something appears. A plume of spray suddenly shoots into the air.

Thar she blows! A whale!

From prehistoric times to the present, the sight of a whale has always quickened the pulse of those who were lucky enough to come into contact with one. Whether you are a seasoned whale expert or a first-time whale watcher, the sighting of a whale never fails to be a thrill.

Thar she blows!

After all, whales are not just the largest creatures ever to live on Earth. They have the biggest brains of any other animal. They

---

THE BLUE WHALE IS THE LARGEST CETACEAN. THE WORD *CETACEAN* COMES FROM THE GREEK WORD, *KETOS*, WHICH MEANS "SEA MONSTER." WHALE IS AN ANGLO-SAXON WORD THAT IS RELATED TO THE WORD WHEEL, DESCRIBING THE WAY A WHALE'S BODY SEEMS TO TURN IN THE WATER.

are the longest, heaviest, loudest, farthest-swimming, deepest-diving animals in the world. They also eat more and grow faster than any other creatures on Earth.

Consider: At a length of up to 110 feet (34 m), a blue whale is the size of three city buses parked end to end, or about 20 feet (6 m) longer than *Diplodocus*, one of the longest dinosaurs. At close to 120 tons (109,000 kg), a blue whale weighs up to eighteen times as much as the largest land animal, the African elephant. The whale's heart is the size of a small car. Its blood vessels are the size of drain pipes. With a tongue that weighs over four tons, a blue whale may take in over 60 tons (54,000 kg) of water at a single gulp! And in a single day, it may eat up to 4 percent of its body weight—almost 5 tons (4,400 kg)!

Now, as the boat gets closer, a dark figure begins to take shape just beneath the surface. It's long, impossibly long, and glides through the water effortlessly, as if to say: "You're not going to rush me!"

Are whales also the most friendly and intelligent, the most musical and mysterious, the most valuable and fiercely hunted animals on the face of the planet? These questions may be a bit more difficult to answer.

Consider: Whales have been hounded, hunted, and slaughtered to near extinction for centuries, yet gray whales, the renowned "devil fish" of the Pacific, are still friendly enough to allow whale watchers to reach out and pat them like house pets.

A single 53-pound (24-kg) chunk of ambergris, a product from the digestive tract of a sperm whale that is used in perfume-making, once sold for over $42,000!

During the nineteenth century, crew members aboard whaling ships would sit in their bunks late at night and hear mysterious singing. These songs would be attributed to ghosts, mermaids, haunted ships, and other supernatural sources. During World War II these same noises interfered with submarine listening posts near Hawaii. In 1967, whale researcher Roger Payne identified the sounds as the songs sung by male humpback whales. A recording of these sounds, *The Songs of the Humpback Whale*, became a best-selling record in 1970, making it the only recording made by non-human performers that has ever topped the music charts.

IN 1851 HERMAN MELVILLE WROTE, "THERE IS NO MEANS KNOWN TO CATCH A FIN WHALE OR ITS FAST [RORQUAL] COUSINS." BUT BY THE END OF THE NINETEENTH CENTURY, FASTER SHIPS AND EXPLOSIVE HARPOONS MADE RORQUAL WHALES EASY TARGETS FOR WHALERS.

On nineteenth century whaling voyages, the capture of one or two whales was valuable enough to pay for an entire three-year journey on the high seas. Yet some whaling ships came home with as many as forty whales in their hold, making their owners rich and their captains well-off. Their crew fared less well, typically accumulating just a few hundred dollars after a voyage that had taken years to complete. On less successful tours, crew members came home with so little that they had no choice but to sign up for the next incredibly difficult and dangerous voyage a short time later.

As the boat gets closer, you begin to understand something about the whale that is perhaps even more amazing than its unbelievable size: it seems to be looking right at you! In fact, the whale may be more curious about you than you are about it!

THOUGH GENTLE AND QUIET, THE GRAY WHALE WAS NICKNAMED THE "DEVIL FISH" FOR ITS FIERCE FIGHTING ABILITY WHEN IT WAS ATTACKED.

And so it goes with whales. They just might be the largest, most amazing, most surprising, most mysterious animals there are.

The whale, having seen enough of its human observers, suddenly turns, rolls, and begins to dive. As its head goes below water, its giant tail flukes rise into the air, breaching above the water for a moment before the whale disappears into the depths.

Whale Tales

Stories of whales date back thousands of years. Unlike most other large sea creatures, whales breathe air. This greatly increased the chances of ancient travelers encountering a whale rather than some other deep-sea creature that didn't need to come up every hour or so. Imagine the surprise of sailors who fished off the coast of Greenland three thousand years ago, when a giant whale suddenly appeared only a few feet from their small boat!

No wonder so many myths, legends, and tales grew up around whales and whaling. Whales were undoubtedly the source behind many accounts in previous centuries of monsters and giant sea serpents that were said to inhabit the ocean and swallow up small boats.

The most famous whale story of all is probably the tale of Jonah in the Bible. Jonah was swallowed by a giant "fish" and lived inside of its belly for three days and nights until the "fish" cast him out on the beach. Impossible? Most likely, yet a more recent account from the 1800s tells of a sailor who was swallowed by a sperm whale and supposedly survived inside of its stomach for several hours. When the whale was killed, the man was said to be released and saved. Is there any truth to this story? It is unlikely that a person could survive inside of a whale without air for longer than a few minutes. Yet strange things do occur in the world, so perhaps this was one of them.

THE OLD TESTAMENT STORY OF JONAH BEING SWALLOWED BY A WHALE HAS BEEN THE SUBJECT OF FASCINATION FOR THOUSANDS OF YEARS.

Dolphins, which are a type of *cetacean*, a group that includes whales and porpoises, occur in the folktales of many cultures. The ancient Greeks and Romans regarded dolphins as very special creatures. Dolphins were thought to be good-natured, fun-loving, and musical. The Greek philosopher Aristotle was among the first to recognize that whales and dolphins were not fish; he correctly classified them as mammals. The Greeks had such affection for dolphins that they made killing one against the law, and labeled it as a crime of murder.

In Japan, the story of the whale and the sea slug is very similar to the familiar tale of the hare and the tortoise. Instead of a rabbit and a tortoise racing, a swift whale and a slow sea slug are matched against one another. The whale speeds from location to location in the race, only to encounter a different sea slug at each place, impersonating the original sea slug, and asking the whale, "What took you so long?"

On islands off the Pacific coast of Canada, the Haida people have many myths and legends that involve whales. In one series of stories, the Haida must battle an enemy that uses killer whales for transportation. Finally, a powerful Haida chief is killed by this enemy and his spirit becomes a killer whale itself. This killer-whale spirit became a beloved figure in the Haida culture. For this reason, the Haida never harm killer whales in any way.

In Europe in the Middle Ages, the tusks of narwhals were sold as unicorn horns and said to have magical properties, including the ability to counteract the effect of any poison. The long, spiraling tusk is actually just a long tooth that looks like a walking stick.

Whaling Begins

While whales were a source of awe in most cases, and a source of fear in others, ancient sailors didn't fail to notice another trait of these giant creatures: they appeared to be easy to kill. In some cases, whales would swim right up to small boats in shallow water. If only there were a way to successfully attack and kill such a huge beast, it would be there for the taking.

In almost every seacoast culture of the world, people eventually figured out a way to hunt and kill whales. The Inuit in northern Canada developed an elaborate sequence of rituals that needed to be followed before whales could be hunted. These rituals involved preparing the boats, the whaling equipment, and the hunters in special ways before they went out to the sea. After the whale was killed its spirit was thanked in a complicated ritual. Prayer was offered to make sure that the whales would return the following year.

In Europe, the twelfth-century Basques of northern Spain were the first to hunt whales on a large-scale basis. The Basques invented many whaling techniques, including the identification of the proper, or "right" whale to hunt. From experience, the Basques learned that with their primitive equipment, blue and fin whales were too big and fast to capture. Sperm whales dived too deep to attach ropes to. Humpback whales were docile and easy to kill, but they sank after they were killed. That left the northern right whale: it was slow; it stayed near the shore line; and it was easy to kill. By the 1500s, the northern right whale became known all over Europe as the "right" whale to kill.

Soon, Britain, Germany, Norway, and the Netherlands had all followed the Basques into whale hunting. The work was treacherous and uncertain, but the rewards were great. A single right whale, or its Arctic cousin, the bowhead whale, was a treasure that would pay for an entire whaling journey. Whales could be used in an astonishing number of ways. The whale's blubber, or fat, could be cooked down into high quality "smoke-less" candles, lamp oil, soaps, and lubricating oils. The great British scientist Sir Isaac Newton read his books by the light of a whale oil lamp in the late 1600s. In the early 1800s, young Abraham Lincoln probably did the same thing in Illinois.

In addition to blubber, whales could be used for a wide variety of other things. The most important whale product was "whale bone," or *baleen*, which was the springy hornlike substance that some whales use to filter their food. Before the age of plastic and spring steel, the remarkable properties of baleen were unmatched in the natural world. It was incredibly strong, yet baleen could bend back over itself and then spring back to its

ALMOST EVERY PART OF THE WHALE HAD SOME PRACTICAL USE.

original position. This made it perfect for such "springy" products as umbrella ribs, brush bristles, watch springs, and the stiffening on women's corsets.

Demand for baleen and other whale products made prices for whales skyrocket. By the early 1600s, populations of right whales in the North Atlantic were dwindling. Norwegian whalers soon traveled to Greenland, where they discovered a new type of whale. The bowhead is a cousin of the right whale that spends all of its time among the ice packs of the Arctic seas. Soon, the rush was on for bowheads and their supply also began to diminish.

Europe's discovery of North America at the end of the fifteenth century opened new whaling waters. By 1640, the New England colonists learned how to hunt whales from the local

Nauset Indians. Before long, ports like New Bedford, Nantucket, and Cold Spring Harbor became bustling whaling centers. By 1750, right whale populations near New England had decreased due to overhunting. Then, by chance, a Nantucket whaling crew was blown off course one day and discovered large groups of sperm whales.

The sperm whale was very different from the right and bowhead whales. It swam faster, dove deeper, and most importantly, it had no baleen around its mouth. But whalers quickly realized that the immense head of the sperm whale was filled with a liquid oil called spermaceti that had many uses. Spermaceti could be made into candles, oils, soaps, and lubricants that were far superior to the fats from any baleen whale.

The hunt for sperm whales began soon. Nantucket became the world's headquarters for sperm whale ships. Whaling continued on the upswing until the 1850s, when it reached its peak. By this time, hundreds of whaling vessels roamed the seven seas of the Earth, hunting almost any whale they could spot. The only great whales that were not hunted were the biggest and swiftest whales of all—the blue whale, fin whale, and sei whale. But by 1870, bomb harpoons and new advances in ship design made *all* whales targets for the whalers.

Over the decades that followed, the hunt turned into a slaughter. During that time, some 350,000 blue whales, 250,000 humpback whales, 750,000 fin whales, and one million sperm whales were killed. The killing continued well into the twentieth century as better and better technology allowed whalers to remove the meat and blubber on what had beome a floating factory in a fraction of the time it had taken fifty years earlier.

Finally in 1931 the first international treaty to limit bowhead whaling was signed. This was followed by bans on killing right whales, blue whales, humpbacks, sei whales, and sperm whales.

In 1841, when Herman Melville was twenty-two, the family business took a turn for the worse. Melville could not find any work. So he did what many young men of that time did: he went to work on a whaling ship. Melville's travels aboard whaling ships in the 1840s became the basis for *Moby Dick*, the now-famous story of the white whale.

Part adventure story, part whaling manual, and part reflection on the nature of good and evil, *Moby Dick* got bad reviews when it was published in 1851. Critics said the book was too long, too technical, and too confusing. Sales were weak. Melville would go on to write other books in the coming years, but he would not be thought of as a successful author—or sell many books—during his lifetime.

After Melville's death in 1891, his books would be completely forgotten for thirty years. Then, in the 1920s, a new group of critics would rediscover Melville. So, about seventy years after publication, *Moby Dick* suddenly became known as a great American masterpiece. Melville's reputation as one of the great masters of literature has continued to this day.

HERMAN MELVILLE'S NOVEL BASED ON HIS 1840S WHALING VOYAGES, *MOBY DICK*, GIVES MODERN READERS A FASCINATING VIEW OF WHAT IT WAS LIKE TO BE A NINETEENTH-CENTURY WHALER.

In 1986, an international treaty that banned all whaling was finally put into place. But centuries of whaling had taken its toll. For example, though the hunting of northern right whales was banned in 1935, now, almost seventy years later, only about three hundred remain—a shockingly low total for a species that once numbered in the hundreds of thousands.

2 What Is a Whale?

Almost 2,400 years ago, the Greek philosopher Aristotle was able to determine that whales were mammals, not fish. How did he reach this conclusion? After all, at first glance, whales seem to have many fishlike characteristics. They live in water and have a smooth, sleek shape. Instead of arms and legs, whales have fins and a sideways tail called a fluke. What makes a cetacean a mammal and not a fish?

First, like other mammals, cetaceans breathe air. They are not able to obtain oxygen from the water, the way fish do. Aristotle must have noticed this trait right off. If whales were fish, why would they need to come up for air? When the bodies of whales and fish were compared, the difference was obvious. Whales had lungs. Fish had gills.

A second key characteristic that cetaceans share with other

THE HUMPBACK WHALE HAS BALEEN AND THROAT GROOVES, SO IT QUALIFIES AS A RORQUAL. HOWEVER, THE HUMPBACK HAS A DIFFERENT BODY SHAPE AND MUCH LARGER FLIPPERS THAN THE OTHER RORQUALS.

THROAT GROOVES AND A SLEEK SHAPE DISTINGUISH THE RORQUALS FROM OTHER GREAT WHALES. THE BLUE WHALE IS THE LARGEST RORQUAL, AND THE LARGEST ANIMAL IN THE WORLD.

mammals is that they are warm-blooded. Warm-blooded animals generate their own body heat. They are called endotherms. Cold-blooded animals such as fish that rely on their environment to obtain heat are called ectotherms.

A third characteristic that whales share with other mammals is their method of reproduction. Fish, reptiles, and many other animal groups reproduce by laying eggs. Cetaceans, on the other hand, give birth to live young like other mammals, and after they are born, whale babies drink their mother's milk.

Fish versus Cetaceans: A Comparison

Fish	Both Fish and Cetaceans	Cetaceans
vertical tail		horizontal tail fluke
scales		smooth skin
gills		lungs
no blowhole		blowhole
	streamlined body	
	underwater habitat	
	no body hair (or little)	
	swimming fins	
cold-blooded		warm-blooded
eggs		live babies
no milk		milk
no care for young		care for their young

Life in the Water

As warm-blooded, milk-giving, air-breathing creatures that give birth to live young, whales in some ways appear to be typical mammals. But in other ways, whales are not typical at all. For example, all other mammals—except whales—have body hair, four limbs (arms and legs), and can breathe through their mouths.

But whales have only two limbs—their front flippers—and no visible body hair. What's more, whales can breathe only through their blowholes. No other mammal shares these features. These differences once again seem to beg the question: are whales really mammals? If so, then why are they so different from other mammals?

In fact, the differences between whales and other mammals—little or no body hair, no rear limbs, and blowholes for breathing—are chiefly products of where whales live. Having moved to an underwater habitat millions of years ago, the whale body form has changed and undergone adaptations that make it better suited to a life in the water.

The ancestors of cetaceans were the small mammals that were first beginning to become widespread on Earth some 65 million years ago—during the time when the dinosaurs disappeared. After the mass extinction of many reptiles at that time, mammals began to move into a variety of new habitats. Most mammals were land animals, but as competition increased, a few mammals moved to the water.

The original whale ancestors lived in shallow river-mouth habitats about 50 million years ago. They were small and looked more like modern-day cattle and sheep than whales. In fact, DNA evidence shows that today's whales are more closely related to hoofed animals than they are to any other living organisms.

Whale Ancestors

ODDLY ENOUGH, THE ANCESTORS OF THE PRESENT-DAY WHALE LIVED ON LAND AND LOOKED A LOT MORE LIKE COWS OR DOGS THAN FISH, AS ONCE BELIEVED.

Why did the original whale ancestors move to the water in the first place? Most likely they were searching for food, avoiding predators, or both. In any event, over millions of years, the whale body changed in several key ways to adapt to living underwater.

The whale's overall body shape became sleek and streamlined for slipping through the water efficiently. Body hair was eliminated except for a few tiny hairs that some whales have near their mouths. Long front legs turned into short flippers. Rear legs disappeared completely. The tail developed into a divided structure called a fluke.

Whales never lost the lungs that they used for breathing on

AT ABOUT TWENTY-SEVEN FEET IN LENGTH, THE MINKE WHALE IS THE SMALLEST OF ALL THE RORQUALS.

land. But the whale's breathing organ, the nose, gradually migrated to the top of the head to become a blowhole. Whales also learned to stay underwater without needing to come up for air. The average human being (also a mammal) can stay underwater for a minute or less. Many whales can stay under for about an hour. Some whales, like the northern bottlenose whale, can stay submerged for up to two hours at a stretch without coming up for air.

Whales also adapted to protect themselves against the cold temperatures of some ocean water, as in the polar latitudes where many whales spend part of their year. To retain body heat, whales developed a thick layer of blubber, or fat, around their bodies. Whales also grew to enormous sizes, which insulated them against the cold.

About 50 million years ago, the first truly whalelike creature emerged. No longer resembling a hoofed land animal, creatures like *Pakicetus* had many of the characteristics of a modern whale. Two adaptations that early whales had not yet developed were

Whale Organs

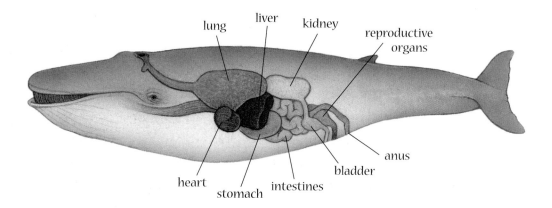

baleen and an echolocation system. The development of these features in some whales created two separate and distinct groups.

Two Types of Whale

Between 25 and 30 million years ago, two critical adaptations arose among the ancestors of modern cetaceans. The first adaptation was baleen, the racks of springy, fringe-covered filters that whales use to strain and capture food. Evidence suggests that even before the development of baleen, some whales were already filtering fish and plankton through their teeth. Once a true baleen system had appeared, however, whales could filter food much more efficiently. Using baleen as a giant strainer, whales could capture thousands of organisms in a single gulp.

While one group of whales developed baleen, a second group gained the ability to locate prey and navigate using *echolocation*. Echolocation works like a sonar system to "see" underwater using sound. To use echolocation, the whale sends out a "signal" wave of sound clicks. The whale then times how long it takes for these clicks to bounce off a distant object—such as a squid—and return. The longer it takes, the farther away the object is. Using echolocation, whales can pinpoint where prey and other objects are located, even in complete darkness. The whales that developed this system suddenly became much more efficient at finding and capturing prey.

These two advances—baleen and echolocation—effectively split whales into two separate groups. The baleen whales make up the *mysticetes*, or "mustached" whale group. Baleen whales are filter feeders that eat plankton (floating organisms) and very small fish. They can be distinguished from toothed whales by their lack of teeth, presence of baleen, and a double, rather than a single, blowhole. The *ondontocetes* are the toothed

Whale Skeleton

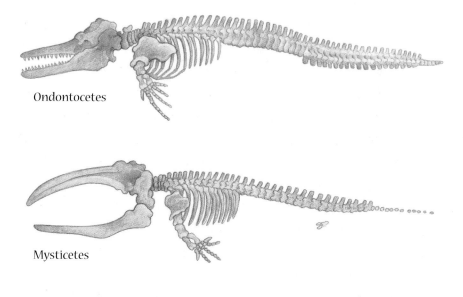

Ondontocetes

Mysticetes

HOW CAN YOU TELL *ONDONTOCETES* FROM *MYSTICETES*? THE ROOT WORD *DONTO* MEANS "TEETH." AS THIS SKELETON SHOWS, THE *ONDONTOCETES*, UNLIKE THE "MUSTACHED" *MYSTICETES*, HAVE TEETH.

whales (a group that includes dolphins and porpoises) that eat larger forms of prey. They can be distinguished from baleen whales by their lack of baleen, the presence of teeth, and a single blowhole. Both baleen whales and toothed whales are members of the group called *cetaceans*.

Baleen Whales	Toothed Whales
Baleen	No baleen
No teeth	Teeth
Eat plankton	Eat bigger prey
Double blowhole	Single blowhole

Baleen Whales

Baleen whales are the giant, gentle "cows" of the ocean. They graze through the water, filtering their food through clattering racks of baleen. The blue whale is a baleen whale. The right whale and humpback are also baleen whales. In all, there are eleven baleen whales that are classified into four families.

The *rorquals* are a family of sleek, swift-swimming giants that come in a range of sizes but all (except the humpback) have the same general shape. Rorquals are distinguished by the horizontal throat grooves that line the bottom of their jaws. These grooves are actually pleats that allow the mouth of a rorqual whale to expand like an accordion and take in enormous quantities of water for filtering.

There are six different rorquals. Five of them—the blue, fin, sei, Bryde's, and minke whale—have the same body shape. The sixth rorqual, the humpback, has a very different body shape. The blue whale is the largest rorqual—and indeed, the largest whale (or animal) in the world. The fin whale looks much like a blue. It is slightly smaller, but still immense, topping out at 78 feet (24 m) in length. The dorsal, or top fin, of the fin whale sticks up a little more prominently than the dorsal fin of a blue whale, and the fin whale's head comes to a sharper V-shaped point when looked at from behind.

The sei whale resembles a fin whale, except that it is generally smaller and avoids the cold polar waters that blue whales and fin whales tend to inhabit. The Bryde's whale is smaller yet, and lives in waters that are almost tropical. Finally, the minke whale is the smallest rorqual of them all, reaching a length of 27 feet (8 m). Minke whales are also called bay whales. The final rorqual is the humpback whale, which has a different body shape and lifestyle than the other rorquals.

Major Types of Whales

Beluga, or white 18 feet (5 m)

Minke 27 feet (8 m)

Pacific Gray 45 feet (14 m)

Humpback 50 feet (15 m)

Sei 60 feet (18 m)

Greenland Right 60 feet (18 m)

Sperm 63 feet (24 m)

Fin 78 feet (24 m)

Blue 100 feet (30.5m)

(Figures are approximate, 1 inch = 30 ft. The figures indicate maximum lengths.)

A second family of baleen whales includes the right whales and bowheads. These slow, bulky creatures can be instantly distinguished from the rorquals in three ways: first, they do not have a dorsal fin on their backs. Second, they tend to have a "bonnet" of growths called *callosities* around their heads. The callosities are often riddled with barnacles and whale lice called amphipods. The third distinguishing feature of a right whale or bowhead is the distinctive fluke displays that these whales make just before they dive.

Right whales and bowheads are closely related, but while right whales live in cold waters just below the Arctic Circle, bowheads prefer to live among the ice packs of the Arctic itself.

And then there are the gray whales. Grays are among the most primitive of whales. They resemble the original ancestors of whales more than any other cetacean. Gray whales are for the most part bottom feeders that stay near shore in the Pacific. Their annual migration from Alaska down the west coast of North America makes them a regular attraction for whale watchers in California and Mexico.

THE SLOWER RIGHT WHALES AND BOWHEADS TEND TO GET UNSIGHTLY CALLOSITIES GROWING ON THEIR HEADS THAT ARE RIDDLED WITH TINY CREATURES.

Toothed Whales

The toothed whales include sperm whales, killer whales, pilot whales, dolphins, narwhals, belugas, and beaked whales. Sperm whales are the largest toothed whales. With their immense heads and huge mouths that appear to be smiling, sperm whales are unlike any other whale. Killer whales are remarkable for their intelligence, loyalty, and hunting skill, including other whales. The killer whale, or *Orcinus orca*, is the largest member of the dolphin family, *Delphinidae*.

THE SNOW WHITE BELUGA IS SOMETIMES CALLED THE "CANARY OF THE SEA" FOR ITS MUSICAL SINGING AND CHIRPING.

Herman Melville took exception to the killer whale's name, saying: "We are all killers, on land and on sea: [Napoleon] Bonaparte and sharks included."

Dolphins and porpoises are the most commonly seen cetacean. The playful, leaping behavior of these creatures has made them a favorite among animal lovers around the world. Narwhals and belugas qualify as some of the most unusual whales. Both live in cold Arctic waters, and both are immediately identifiable—narwhals from their single unicornlike horn, and belugas from their snow white color.

Though there are nineteen different species of beaked whale, very little is known about this cetacean group. Many have never been seen alive, while others are observed only rarely. One reason why beaked whales are so seldom seen is that they spend almost all of their time in the open ocean, never coming close to land.

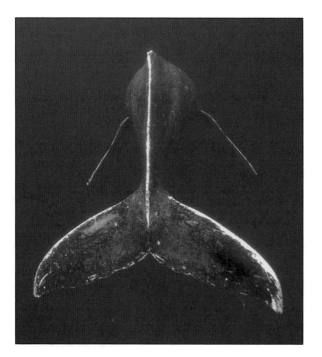

Because of its easy-going nature and regular appearances at certain locations, the southern right whale has been called the easiest whale to study.

TIMELINE

210 million years ago	● First mammals
50 million years ago	● First cetacean ancestor
46–50 million years ago	● *Pakicetus*, first whale
35–50 million years ago	● Whale body shape changes: flipper, blowhole, and fluke develop; body hair and hind limbs disappear; shape streamlined
30–40 million years ago	● First baleen whales
25 million years ago	● First cetaceans with echolocation
20 million years ago	● Sperm whales appear
12–15 million years ago	● First dolphins
4 million years ago	● Original cetacean ancestors disappear

Modern Times

1832	● Basilosaurus—whale ancestor fossil found
1900	● Northern right whale almost extinct
1904	● Huge populations of humpbacks, blues, fins, Southern rights, and seis found near Antarctica
1925–1940	● 750,000 fin whales, 360,000 blues slaughtered in southern oceans
1996	● 81 different whale species recognized
2002	● Just over 300 Northern right whales still exist

WHALES HAVE EXISTED FOR MILLIONS OF YEARS. WHILE WHALE-WATCHING HAS BECOME A FORM OF RECREATION IN RECENT YEARS, FEWER AND FEWER WHALES REMAIN ALIVE, DESPITE BANS AGAINST HUNTING THEM.

3 Inside a Whale

When whales took to the water millions of years ago, they encountered a whole new set of problems and conditions. Living in water was very different than living on land. Most of the differences were due to the properties of water itself. How do these properties affect the way a whale sees, feels, and moves through its environment? Consider: Water is almost eight hundred times as heavy as air. Water absorbs heat twenty-seven times faster than air. Water blocks much more of the sun's energy than air. (At a depth of 33 feet [10 meters], water blocks 90 percent of the sun's light.) Water transmits sound waves about 4.5 times faster than air. Finally, while both water and air create pressure, the extra weight of water results in deep sea pressures that dwarf any air pressure felt on land.

How do these properties of water affect whales? In almost every way, whales are built to live in water. Their body size, shape,

THE TAIL FLUKE POWERS THE WHALE THROUGH THE WATER. NOTICE THAT THE FLUKE IS ORIENTED IN A HORIZONTAL (SIDEWAYS) DIRECTION WHILE THE TAIL OF A FISH HAS A VERTICAL (UP AND DOWN) ORIENTATION.

and surface are perfectly suited to a life in a medium that is thicker, heavier, colder, darker, and more supportive than air. Their internal organization is also perfectly suited to a salt water habitat.

The only feature of the ocean that whales do not seem to be able to take advantage of is its oxygen. While oxygen is plentiful in the ocean, whales are unable to make use of it for breathing because they do not have gills, so they must periodically come up for air. Whales may in every way look and act like creatures of the sea, but ultimately they are still connected to the world above the water.

Underwater Adaptation 1: Body Size (Bigger Is Better)

On land, an animal is a prisoner of its own weight. The larger an animal gets, the more difficult it becomes to support itself. For example, imagine two whales, one twice the size of the other.

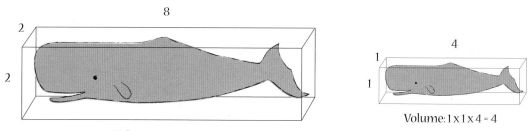

Volume: 2 x 2 x 8 = 32

Volume: 1 x 1 x 4 = 4

As the measurements in the above diagram show, the larger whale is twice as long, twice as wide, and twice as thick as the smaller whale. You might expect the larger whale to weigh twice as much as the smaller whale. In fact, the larger whale would weigh eight times as much as the smaller whale. To see why, take a look at the diagrams on page 38 and on this page. The box that the large whale fits into is eight times as large as the small whale's box. It stands to reason that the large whale would be eight times as heavy.

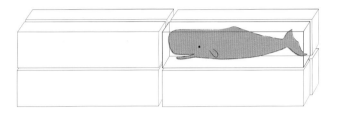

On land, this extra weight can pose a big problem. If an elephant doubles in size, its bones can't just double in strength—they need to get eight times as strong to support its new weight. As land animals get larger and larger, supporting body weight becomes a bigger and bigger concern. That is why the biggest land animals—such as elephants, and hippos—have such thick bones. They need to support a huge amount of weight.

In water, however, weight is not much of a problem. Things don't weigh much in water because the water itself supports their weight. Archimedes, another ancient Greek scientist, was the first to understand how fluids affect weight. According to Archimedes, when an object is placed in a fluid, it is pushed up with a force that is equal to the weight of the liquid it displaces (pushes aside).

For example, a balloon filled with 1 liter of air would displace 1 liter (1,000 g) of water if it were pushed beneath the surface. Since a liter of air weighs just 0.044 ounces (1.25 grams), it would be pushed up by the far greater 2.2-pound (1,000-g) force of the displaced water, making it float.

1.25 g
force

1.25 g
air

1,000 g
force

Balloon displaces 1,000 g of water

FLOATS

1,200 g
force

sand

1,000 g
force

SINKS

1,000 g
force

air
+ water

1,000 g
force

DRIFTS

Now fill a second balloon with 2.6 pounds (1,200 g) of sand. The sand-filled balloon weighs more than the 2.2 pounds (1,000 g) of water it displaces, so it sinks.

Now fill a third balloon with both water and air so that it weighs 2.2 pounds (1,000 g). This balloon has the exact same weight as the water it displaces. So it drifts—neither floating nor sinking. Take some of the air out and it will sink. Put some extra air in and it will float to the surface.

A whale is like this third balloon. Its density is about the same as the density of water. It can float, sink, or drift, depending on how much air it takes in. A whale is almost "weightless" in water because its huge volume is supported by a force that is equal to the weight of the water it displaces.

To understand this "weightlessness," think of how easy it is to lift a friend in a swimming pool. The friend seems almost "weightless" to you, because he or she is being supported by the water. How does this "weightlessness" affect whales? It allows them to grow to enormous sizes without growing large bones to support their weight. In fact, the bones of whales are soft and full of holes. They don't need to be nearly as strong as the bones of land animals, because they support much less real weight.

Underwater Adaptation 2: Getting Around

Air is so thin compared to water that it provides almost no resistance. Try flapping your arms up and down. Does it propel you upward in any way? Now try the same thing underwater. Flapping your arms against a medium that pushes back produces results. You move up and down in the water.

On land, the secret to locomotion is to focus effort on a single spot against a solid object. Thus, a pole vaulter gets maximum height by pushing down against the ground at a single focused location. When you run, you do pretty much the same thing—

SLOWER WHALES, LIKE THIS SOUTHERN RIGHT WHALE, TEND TO HAVE LARGER RACKS OF BALEEN.

your feet focus your muscle effort on a single spot, allowing you to push against the ground for maximum speed.

In water, you don't need to push against solid objects. You can push against the water itself for locomotion. Rather than focus your effort in a single spot, you want to broaden it so you are pushing against a maximum amount of water in a single stroke.

For a whale, a flipper or fluke does this job nicely. To propel itself forward, the flipper pushes against a broad area of water to get a maximum push. The return stroke cuts through the water as thinly as possible to prevent the animal from slowing down.

The whale's tail fluke is its main organ of locomotion. It sweeps out at a huge area of water to propel the whale forward. Notice that fish and whales do not use the same basic swimming method. A fish uses its muscular body to propel itself, moving its vertical tail from side to side. A whale's fluke moves up and down like a paddle. This up-and-down motion is what powers the whale forward. The whale's flippers are used primarily for steering and braking.

In practice, the whale moves very efficiently through the water. Three evolutionary adaptations are largely responsible for this efficiency. First, the whale's forelimbs changed shape to become flippers instead of legs. The rear limbs, on the other hand, disappeared—almost completely. An examination of a whale's skeleton shows that the tiny, unseen rear limb bones still exist, but they no longer have any practical function.

A closer look at the whale's flippers shows both how much—and how little—they have changed over millions of years when compared to other mammals. With respect to shape and function, a dolphin's flipper and a human arm couldn't seem more different. Yet in structure the two limbs match up almost perfectly—joint for joint and bone for bone. It seems likely that

AT A DEPTH OF 33 FEET (10 M), WATER BLOCKS ABOUT 90 PERCENT OF THE SUN'S LIGHT.

at one point in time, both limbs might have been very similar.

A third major adaptation that whales have for underwater locomotion is a streamlined body shape. On land, streamlining is not a very big issue for most animals at low speeds. As you run, the air drags against your body, slowing you down. But the air is so thin that the effect is quite minor.

In water, a much thicker medium, drag is a serious problem. To minimize drag, whales took on a sleek, streamlined body shape. They also lost all of their body hair. As a result, whales have the smoothest skin of all mammals. Many people who have felt the skin of a live whale compare it in smoothness to the skin of a baby.

Underwater Adaptation 3: Staying Warm

Imagine living in a medium in which you lose heat twenty-seven times faster than you do in air. Then factor in the year-round cold temperatures of the polar oceans, the habitat in which many great whales spend much of their time. How do whales stay warm?

The most important "whale warmer" is the blubber that covers the body of almost every whale. Blubber is a type of fat, and fat is a good insulator. In essence, blubber works the way a warm coat works. The thicker the coat, the more heat it keeps in. Cold water whales such as the bowhead can have as much

as 20 inches (50 cm) of blubber around their bodies. Most other whales have a blubber layer that is about 4 to 7 inches (12 to 18 cm) thick.

To understand how blubber warms, think back to the small and large whale on pages 38 and 39. The small whale loses heat much faster than the large whale. To understand why, suppose you have a whole deep dish pizza and a single slice of the same pizza sitting on the table in front of you. Both are bubbling hot. Which will get cold faster?

The slice and the small whale proportionally have more surface area relative to their body size that is exposed to the air. Since they have more surface area than the whole pizza and the large whale, they lose heat faster. So a larger-sized animal holds heat longer—and that includes whales.

Underwater Adaptation 4: Pressure and Breathing

As a whale dives deeper, the weight of the water above begins to add up. On a solid (or liquid-filled) body part, water pressure doesn't have much effect—first, because solids and liquids aren't compressible and second, because the pressure from the water above gets canceled out by pressure from water below (and on all sides, actually). A solid body part is squeezed, but it is squeezed fairly evenly on all sides, so damage is minimal.

The only place where pressure can be fully felt is in body spaces that are open and contain gas, which is very compressible. Your ears, for example, have empty space in them, so they tend to hurt if you dive deeply underwater without protection. Gas that normally exists in solution in body fluids can also cause trouble. One particular gas, nitrogen, can cause a condition known as the *bends*, or decompression sickness. To understand what causes the bends, think of a bottle of soda pop. It is bottled

THE SPERM WHALE HAS EIGHTEEN PAIR OF LARGE, PEGLIKE TEETH. THIS IS FEWER THAN MOST TOOTHED WHALES.

under pressure—that is, gas is forced into the liquid, where it stays in solution when the bottle is capped. When the cap is taken off, the pressure on the liquid is suddenly gone. Now, gas starts bubbling out of the liquid.

A similar thing happens when a scuba diver comes up too quickly. Pressurized nitrogen that the diver breathed in comes out of solution in the diver's blood, forming bubbles in the joints and other areas when he surfaces. These bubbles can cause extreme pain, sickness, and other serious symptoms.

How do cetaceans avoid the bends? Scientists aren't sure, but they suspect that they do it in three ways. First, the nitrogen that whales breathe in (air is almost 80 percent nitrogen) isn't pressurized like nitrogen from a tank. Second, and more importantly, whales appear not to take in much air when they dive. Evidence shows that whales collapse their lungs during a deep dive, which means they have little internal gas of any type to compress. Finally, whales appear to reduce blood flow, which keeps bubbling to a minimum.

The method whales use for avoiding the bends brings up a new problem: if whales don't take much air down with them when they dive, how do they stay down for so long? In fact, all animals need oxygen. They use it to burn fuel (food) to get energy—in much the same way that a fire uses oxygen to burn wood and release energy.

When we go underwater for more than a few seconds we come up gasping for oxygen. How can whales stay down so long without coming up to get oxygen themselves?

Again, scientists aren't sure that they know the full story of how whales can stay underwater for prolonged periods. What is known can be summarized by the following four points. First,

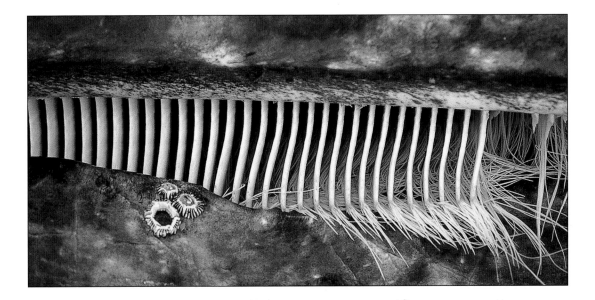

WHALE WATCHERS SOMETIMES CAN HEAR THE RATTLE OF THE BALEEN PLATES AS THE WHALE CLEARS ITS MOUTH.

when a whale dives it slows down all of its body functions except in those places where function is really needed. The heart rate drops, as well as blood flow to many body areas, such as the digestive system. This reduces the need for oxygen.

Second, rather than store oxygen in the blood, the whale stores much of its oxygen in its muscles. Whale muscle looks black, indicating that it is full of myoglobin, a chemical that is much like the hemoglobin that holds oxygen in human blood. By storing oxygen in the muscles where it is needed rather than in the blood, the whale again gains time in staying underwater.

Third, the buildup of carbon dioxide (the end product of breathing oxygen) in human blood is a trigger that forces you to take a breath. That is, if you hold your breath for a long time, carbon dioxide builds up in your blood. That buildup induces a gasping reflex that forces you to try to breathe, even if you're underwater. Whales are much more tolerant of carbon dioxide buildup than humans and can go much longer without gasping.

Fourth, when humans use up all of the oxygen in their blood they switch to a "no oxygen" anaerobic way to get energy. Anaerobic metabolism is a way of burning food to get energy without using oxygen. Humans can burn fuel anaerobically if they need to. But prolonged anaerobic metabolism results in a buildup of lactic acid in the blood, which causes muscle cramps and other problems. Whales have a system that is much more tolerant of lactic acid buildup than other mammals have. This allows them to stay underwater for longer periods of time.

Underwater Adaptation 5: Navigating the Darkness

As mentioned above, many whales spend most of their time in a semi-dark, or completely dark environment. Sperm whales, for example, dive to depths of 3,300 feet (1,000 m) and greater, far below the level at which even the slightest glimmer of light penetrates.

How do whales get around this dark environment? For the most part, they rely on their sense of sound. Sperm whales and other toothed whales have an *echolocation* system that allows them to use sound clicks to locate objects in the darkness. Baleen whales do not use echolocation, but they do take advantage of the rapid speed at which sound travels underwater—at around 3,355 miles (5,400 km) per hour (four to five times faster than sound in air) to sense things in their world and to communicate.

4 Whales in Action

Whales are the biggest food consumers in the entire animal kingdom. How important is food to a whale? During its short five-month feeding season, a blue whale may eat up to 4 percent of its entire body weight each day—or almost 5 tons (4,400 kg) of food in a single day for a whale that weighs 120 tons (109,000 kg)!

Where do whales find so much food, and how do they manage to swallow it all? In fact, baleen and toothed whales have very different methods of obtaining food. Though they both eat animals (not plants), baleen whales are the "grazers" of the oceans, filtering through vast feeding waters, devouring unimaginable quantities of tiny creatures. Toothed whales hunt rather than graze, but they too must consume huge quantities of food to satisfy their basic daily energy requirements.

HUMPBACKS ARE THE ONLY WHALES THAT USE THEIR FLIPPERS TO HERD PREY DURING FEEDING.

The Prey: Krill

In the cold waters of the polar regions at either end of the globe, every spring brings an explosion of growth. These are the richest ocean waters in the world. Enormous swarms of small creatures called *krill* wriggle on or near the surface of the water. At one location, an estimated 2.5 million tons (2.3 billion kg) of krill gathered together in a single super-swarm. That's some 5 billion pounds of krill, or about 50 billion individual animals in a single gathering.

Krill is a term that is often used to describe any smallish crustaceanlike creature that inhabits the oceans. Technically speaking, krill refers to a species of creatures called *euphausiids* that measure about 2.4 inches (6 cm) in length and resemble shrimp.

SHRIMPLIKE KRILL MEASURE ABOUT 2.4 INCHES (6 CM) IN LENGTH.

While krill are found in other parts of the world, they are most abundant in nutrient-rich polar waters. What makes these waters so productive? In fact, you might expect that warm tropical waters near the equator would support the most life. But tropical waters stay pretty much the same temperature all year around. This creates permanent layers of warm and cold water in the tropics that never mix. Since warm water is less dense, it tends to rise, leaving a layer of cold water below. The result is that the warm upper layers never get to mix with the nutrient-rich waters below.

In polar regions, surface waters get very cold in the winter, and sink. They sink so far that they mix with deeper, nutrient-rich waters below. In the spring, winds and turbulence bring these mixed waters upward. The nutrients that they contain are consumed by enormous blooms of algae. The algae, in turn, are eaten by krill, which itself becomes food for baleen whales.

Baleen Whale Feeding: Gulpers, Skimmers, and Others

Imagine that krill were considered to be edible seafood for human consumption, like shrimp. At about ten dollars a pound (about half a kg) for shrimp, a single whale could consume almost $100,000 worth of food each day!

Different baleen whales have different feeding methods. The two most common methods are gulping and skimming. Most of the throat-grooved rorquals (blue, fin, sei, Bryde's, minke) are "gulpers" who use their expandable, pouchlike lower jaw to take in huge quantities of water.

The slower right whales and bowheads are "skimmers" that trawl through the depths with their mouths open, taking in water and prey continuously. Gray whales (and some bow-heads) are bottom feeders that bulldoze their way along the

BALEEN WHALES GENERALLY HAVE TWO DIFFERENT FEEDING STYLES. THE FAST
RORQUALS, LIKE THIS BLUE WHALE, ARE GULPERS. THEIR THROAT GROOVES ALLOW
THEM TO EXPAND THEIR MOUTHS AND TAKE IN HUGE QUANTITIES OF WATER. THE
SLOWER GRAYS AND RIGHTS ARE SKIMMERS.

ocean floor, filtering out all but the tiny krill-like creatures that
they find edible.

While humpback whales are technically rorquals (because
they have throat grooves) their feeding methods are markedly
different from other baleen whales. Humpbacks engage in all
sorts of tactics to capture prey, including lunge feeding, flick
feeding (creating a wave of water with the flick of the tail), and
"herding" prey into clusters by smacking the water. Humpbacks
also work together to create *bubble nets*—large columns of
water bubbles—to round up prey into groups for swallowing.

While right whales, gray whales, bowhead, rorquals, and

humpbacks all seem to feed in different ways, they do have one very important feature in common: baleen. Baleen is an amazingly strong and springy material. Before the age of plastics, this so-called "whalebone" was the most treasured part of a baleen whale's body. Indeed, in 1859, when large quantities of underground petroleum oil were discovered in Pennsylvania, demand

To form bubble nets, humpbacks swim upward in a spiral pattern, releasing bubbles at precise locations along the way. The tube of bubbles herds the prey together so it can be easily snatched up.

for whale oil immediately dropped, but the public's appetite for baleen to make such things as umbrella spokes, corsets, brushes, and fishing rods continued to be strong. In fact, right whales and other baleen species were hunted almost to extinction well into the twentieth century—even though petroleum oil had for the most part replaced whale oil. It was only after the invention of spring steel in 1908 that demand for whalebone finally began to diminish.

Different whales have different kinds of baleen. The skimmers and bottom feeders—right whales, bowheads, and gray whales—have the most elaborate baleen formations. The bowhead has the greatest number of baleen plates, up to 330 in each animal. Each plate is a long, triangle-shaped rack that hangs down from the whale's upper jaw like a huge curtain. (Baleen plates are not teeth; baleen whales do not have teeth, except as embryos.) The whalebone part of the plate is made of hard keratin, the same material that is used to make fingernails and animal horns.

Beneath the hard, springy keratin lies a veil of hairlike fringe. This is the material on which small prey animals are actually caught. The gray whale's baleen has the finest-gauge fringe, probably because, as a bottom feeder, it eats the tiniest animals. Humpback whales, who eat larger fish species, have much coarser fringe.

A Rorqual Meal

The actual tracking down of krill by rorquals and other baleen whales is somewhat of a mystery. How do rorquals, such as the blue whale, detect the presence of prey in the water? Do they smell their prey? Most whale experts are doubtful that whales employ—or even possess—much of a sense of smell at all.

Vision is also a fairly unreliable sense in the water, which can be murky, and below 66 feet (20 m) or so, quite dark. Tasting the water might be more likely. In fact, rorquals, like cats, are equipped with something called a Jacobsen's organ. This is the same sensory organ that snakes use to "taste" the air to detect the presence of enemies and prey.

Rorquals also may use the tiny one-half-inch-long hairs they have on their bodies to sense vibrations and disturbances in the water that krill and other creatures make. In any event, the whale

THE SPRINGY WHALEBONE THAT WAS ONCE USED TO MAKE UMBRELLAS MERELY PROVIDES THE FRAMEWORK FOR BALEEN. THE PREY ITSELF IS TRAPPED ON THESE FURRY BRISTLES.

somehow manages to use one of its senses—or a combination of senses—to locate swarms of prey in the water. Once detected, the whale swims over to the swarm and takes a huge gulp. As its mouth fills, the rorqual's throat pleats spread out to their maximum size, expanding to hold an immense quantity of water. It has been estimated that a blue whale can take in more than 60 tons (54,000 kg) of water in a single gulp!

After gulping, the whale's mouth closes and the tongue pushes up, forcing the water out through the baleen, trapping the organisms that are left behind. The tongue of a rorqual is an amazing organ, weighing in at up to 4 tons (3,600 kg) for a blue whale, and having the texture of a jelly-filled balloon.

Once the water is forced out of the mouth, the whale proceeds to swallow the creatures left behind through a tiny gullet that measures only a few inches across. If this sounds amazing to

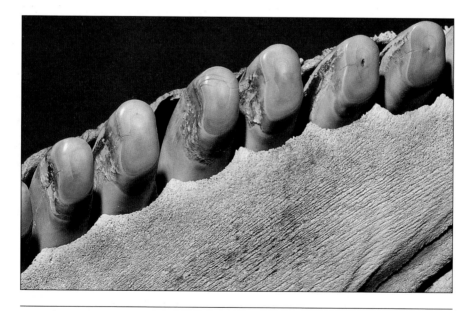

TOOTHED CETACEANS, LIKE THIS KILLER WHALE, HAVE MORE TEETH THAN ANY OTHER MAMMAL.

you, you are not alone. Scientists are still puzzled by how a rorqual, or other baleen whales, can take in so much food through such a small opening. One estimate shows that the whale must pass 160 pounds (73 kg) of krill down its throat for each gulp it takes in.

Toothed Whale Feeding: Hunters of the Deep

The difference between a toothed whale and a baleen whale can be best appreciated by looking into the mouth of each type of whale. Baleen whales have no teeth. Toothed whales—which include sperm whales, killer whales, beaked whales, and dolphins, have dozens of peglike, cone-shaped teeth. In fact, they have more teeth than any other mammal.

The sperm whale, the greatest of the toothed whales, is also one of the most mysterious when it comes to hunting. With its huge mouth, the sperm whale is known to be a hunter of squid and deep-sea fish. Many whale yarns tell of legendary battles between giant squid and sperm whales. While these battles undoubtedly must have occurred, they were probably more one-sided than the storytellers would like to admit. The largest squid ever found was just over 39 feet (12 meters) in body length and must have weighed only a small fraction of the 50 or so tons that a typical sperm whale weighs. Rather than a fair fight, sperm whale–giant squid battles were probably little more than a desperate and usually unsuccessful struggle on the squid's part to escape from its captor.

In fact, squid make up the majority of a sperm whale's diet. One estimate indicates that a typical large sperm whale devours up to a ton (900 kg) of squid each day. The average squid is probably no more than 3.3 feet (1 meter) or so in length. How are sperm whales able to track down so much food? While the details are not known for sure, scientists do know that sperm whales dive deep to find their prey—deeper than any other whale, perhaps more than a mile (1,600 m) down in some instances.

At this depth, the sperm whale swims in absolute darkness. Echolocation, however, gives the whale a reliable picture of its environment. How accurate is this picture? Consider some experiments done during the 1950s with dolphins, other toothed whales that use echolocation. These experiments showed that the dolphins could swim freely while blindfolded and easily avoid obstacles at high speed. In a different experiment, the dolphins were also able to detect targets that measured only 0.08 inches (2 mm) across, again while blindfolded.

No one questions that echolocation is reliable for navigating underwater and locating prey. The way sperm whales and other toothed cetaceans actually use their echolocation is less clear. Thomas Beale, author of the 1899 book *Natural History of the Sperm Whale*, describes a living sperm whale's tongue as "being of a glistening white color . . ." that mesmerizes and lures in its prey.

Some whale experts think that instead of chasing after individual squid—a tiresome exercise for such a small reward, in most instances—sperm whales may first use a strong pulse of echolocation clicks to stun their prey, then employ a surge of suction to suck the victim into their open mouth.

In any event, echolocation is used not just by sperm whales, but by every deep-diving toothed cetacean, including killer whales and dolphins. In most cases, the whale sends out a series of high-frequency signal clicks, probably from its melon, a spongy, liquid-filled area of the head, as it makes its way through its environment. Then the whale guages the location of and distance to the prey based on how long it takes for the signal clicks to return from a target object.

1 mile

2 seconds

In the top example, an object 1 mile (1,600 m) away would take about 2 seconds to travel to its target and return. A signal that took only half as long to return (below) would be sensed by the whale to be only half as far away. By constantly monitoring and fine-tuning its signal click, the whale can get an accurate image of its surroundings. Sound transmission is up to 4.5 times faster underwater than it is through the air. In the air, an object 1 mile (1,600 m) away would take about 9 seconds to return sound, rather than 2 seconds.

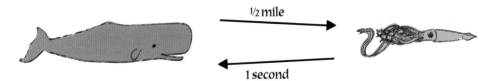

½ mile

1 second

While sperm whales usually hunt on their own, killer whales, also known as orcas, often hunt in groups. There is evidence that orcas actually have "jobs" to do as they attack a group of minke whales in an attempt to grab one of the babies. The older orcas will distract the adult minke whales, while the younger attackers come in to take the prey. While many whale experts feel orcas rarely kill other whales, they are sure that orcas are the only cetaceans that eat other mammals.

Indeed, orcas are known to eat sea birds, marine mammals such as seals, otters, and porpoises, and even land animals such as caribou that happen to wander too closely to the shore. Orcas are also known for their clever hunting techniques. In the water, they work together to herd a school of fish into a tight ball before attacking. Killer whales are even known to come up on dry land and snatch baby seals from the beach.

5 Migration and Life Cycle

Each year, when the polar ice caps begin to melt, the whales arrive in the Arctic seas of both the Northern and Southern Hemispheres. Some, like the humpbacks and gray whales, may have traveled thousands of miles to reach their destination. In fact, humpback whales migrate farther than any other land or sea animal, traveling over 5,000 miles (8,000 km) one way in some cases. The pattern is similar for most other baleen whales. After a winter in warm waters, they head off north (or in the Southern Hemisphere, south) to their feeding waters. What drives these whales to travel so far?

The simplest explanation for baleen whale migration is that the whales are hungry. In fact, many baleen whales spend the entire winter warm-water season without eating at all. So they are drawn to the food-rich polar regions, whose waters bloom each year with an explosion of *plankton*. Plankton is a term that includes all life-forms that drift, rather than actively swim, in the

RORQUAL WHALES SPEND THE ENTIRE SUMMER SEASON IN POLAR REGIONS, GORGING THEMSELVES ON FOOD.

ocean. The cycle begins with the growth of one-celled plants called algae. Algae serves as the main food source for small fish, copepods, and crustaceans that include the shrimplike euphausiids, krill.

As soon as the whales arrive in their feeding waters, they begin hungrily taking in huge volumes of krill and other foods. Many of them have a lot of eating to do. A female humpback or gray whale may lose up to 50 percent of her body weight over the winter season, as a result of giving birth, nursing her baby, and not eating for several months. During the short polar feeding season, she must replenish her body by taking in immense quantities—literally tons—of food each day.

The goal for these creatures is not just to reach a moderate size, but to put on extra weight as body fat (blubber) that can be used as an energy source for the following year. In fact, whales are a bit like squirrels, in that during the summer they store away food for the following winter. But rather than put food away in hiding places, whales store it in the most handy place of all—their own bodies. Blubber, for a whale, serves two purposes. First, it provides a layer of insulation to keep the whale warm. Second, it provides a place to store food energy as body fat that can be used when food is not available. Your own body actually works the same way. If, for some reason, you go without eating for a period of time, your body will start breaking down its own fat stores for energy. Humans, for the most part, want to minimize the amount of body fat they carry because they have access to a source of food each day. Whales, on the other hand, need to plan for a prolonged period of not eating, so they have to carry as much blubber as possible.

For most baleen, and some toothed, whales, the year is sharply divided along seasonal boundaries. In the summer, whales spend their time in cold polar waters where they do little

OF ALL THE GREAT WHALES, HUMPBACKS PUT ON THE BEST SHOWS OF BREACHING,
OR JUMPING OUT OF THE WATER. SOME SCIENTISTS THINK THAT BREACHING IS A
FORM OF COMMUNICATION.

else but gorge themselves. In their warmer winter homes,
whales mate and give birth but eat little or not at all.

What signals do whales receive in the spring that suddenly

tell them it is time to pack up and head to the Arctic? Scientists suspect that:

1. Whales may detect differences in the sun's angle.

2. Whales may detect differences in water temperature as spring begins.

3. Whales may have some internal "clock" in their bodies that tells them when it's time to migrate, based, for example, on how much body fat they still have.

A more basic question, perhaps, would address the general idea of whale migration itself. On the surface, migration may seem like a natural and obvious feature of the whale's life style. But the more you look at whale migration, the more puzzling it becomes, until ultimately you might ask: Why do whales migrate at all?

Why Do Whales Migrate?

For animals like birds, migration seems to make perfect sense. A robin, for example, spends the summer in the north where it is warm and green. By late fall, with food sources harder and harder to come by, the robin migrates south to an environment that is warm and provides plenty of food. When it returns in the spring, the robin finds its northern home replenished—full of green plants and the insects that feed on them.

At first glance, whale migration seems to make sense in the same way. Whales (in the Northern Hemisphere) go south in the winter, and head back north in the spring. But there is one important difference: robins eat in their winter homes; whales don't eat. In fact, since most whales don't consume any food at all in

A SPERM WHALE CALF ALMOST NEVER GETS FAR FROM ITS MOTHER OR OTHER ADULT.

their tropical winter homes, why don't they just save themselves the trip and stay in the polar waters all year round?

One possible reason to migrate is for breeding purposes. Perhaps whale calves (baby whales), being much smaller and less protected by blubber than adults, are not able to tolerate the cold waters of the polar seas just after they are born. This idea seems to make sense until you recognize that many whales do breed in cold polar waters. Among them are bowhead, narwhals, belugas, and some orca (killer whale) populations. And many smaller, less well-insulated animals also stay in the Arctic year round, such as seals and walruses. So why would baleen whales, which are greater in size and better insulated than any of the species that stay near the Pole all year round, need to leave?

Another possible reason for migration is to save energy. If they wintered in their cold-water homes, whales would burn up huge amounts of energy just keeping warm in the cold climate. So they go south to warm waters where they don't need to burn energy just to keep up their body temperature. This seems plausible. But when you think about all the energy whales must burn to travel thousands of miles to warmer waters, and all the energy they use not eating for several months, the idea seems less and less convincing.

In the end, scientists aren't sure why whales migrate. They also aren't sure why some whales always migrate, others sometimes migrate, and still others don't migrate at all. For example, among baleen whales, gray whales and the rorquals (except for Bryde's whales) are the most reliable migrators. Gray whales are probably more regular than any other species, showing up just like clockwork at the same locations off the southern California coast and in Baja, Mexico, during the winter months. Humpback migration is also extremely predictable in most cases. On the other hand, Bryde's whale is a small rorqual that doesn't migrate

at all. It spends its entire year in warm waters, and never ventures to the cold water feeding grounds that other rorquals frequent. The bowhead, the Arctic cousin of the right whale, is pretty much the opposite of Bryde's whale—staying north all year, migrating only as far as the edge of the polar ice pack. As the ice moves south in winter, the bowhead migrates south. When the ice retreats north in summer, it moves north. Right whales are also slow and irregular migrators that tend not to move very far most years.

The toothed whales are less regular and reliable migrators than most baleen whales. Sperm whales, for example, may travel thousands of miles during some years to polar waters. Then, at other times, they will remain in warm waters for several years in a row. The flexibility of toothed whales is closely connected to their ability to obtain food. Many baleen whales, such as humpbacks and grays, find it absolutely necessary to return to the

Arctic to fatten up on krill. Sperm whales can apparently find enough deep-water squid and other prey to stay in warm or temperate water locations year-round, if they need to.

Other toothed species such as orcas and dolphins do not migrate at all. Some nonmigrating species live in year-round cold-water locations, while others live in warm-water locations year-round.

KILLER WHALES ARE FOUND ALL OVER THE WORLD. THEY CAN BREED IN BOTH WARM AND COLD WATERS.

A Year as a Whale

The seasons play a major role in the lives of almost all baleen whales, and many toothed whales as well. In some ways, whales follow a yearly "calendar" more strictly than people do. While people celebrate special days of the year, whales "observe" similar occasions that mark, for example, the day when they begin to head south, move north, and so on.

A year in the life of a blue whale begins in the warm breeding waters of the south. The pregnant female, who successfully mated with a male a year earlier, has now returned to the same waters to give birth to her calf. Over the winter she fattened herself up to an enormous size, getting ready for the hardship ahead. Her last gulp of food took place upon leaving the polar feeding waters in the fall. From here on in, she will not eat again for months, until she migrates back to the north with her newborn calf.

Once born, the baby will suffer no such lack of nourishment. In fact, it will eat almost continuously over the next few months, gaining as much as 180 pounds (86 kg) of body weight each day. That's almost 8 pounds (3.6 kg) per hour! To gain this much weight, the calf feeds exclusively on its mother's super-rich milk, which, ounce for ounce, has ten times the food energy value as cow's milk. Meanwhile, the mother will go day after day without taking in a single calorie of food.

Most baleen whale calves nurse for a year or less. During that first year, calves enjoy a very special relationship with their mother. For southern right whales, the sense of touch seems especially important, as the mother continually rolls her child over, nuzzles it, and holds it in her flippers. This close relationship lasts for one complete migration cycle. When the whales return from their Antarctic feeding waters the following year, all nursing and nuzzling ends. The calf, now a young whale, is on its own.

In general, baleen whales are much less social than toothed whales. After their first year of life, baleen whales seem to keep to themselves as a group while traveling to and from the feeding waters each year. Toothed whales, on the other hand, are highly social. Groups stay close together, never very far out of contact. For sperm whales and bottlenose dolphins, mother-child relationships last for years, often until the offspring are ready to reproduce on their own. In the case of pilot whales and

killer whales, bonds formed early in life may last a lifetime.

After infancy, most whales become part of a group called a pod. Baleen whale pods are fairly loose and informal. For toothed whales such as sperm whales, pilot whales, dolphins, and orcas, pods can be very close and well-organized. Orcas seem to have some of the tightest pods. Among orcas, each core pod group can have two to nine members. At various times, core groups then join together with other core groups to form larger "super-pod" groups of sixty or more animals.

Baleen whales are ready to reproduce when they reach the age of five to seven. Toothed whales generally take much longer to mature. Orcas and bottlenose dolphins may not mature until they are ten years or older. Male sperm whales may not join in the mating process until they reach their middle to late twenties.

Every whale species has its own unique mating behavior, but all whales seem to share a few general characteristics. No whale species mates for life. In most cases, either males have more than one female partner (sperm whales, humpbacks, narwhals, orcas) or both males and females have more than one partner (gray whales, right whales, bowheads). This is a typical pattern for most mammal species.

Mating is typically preceded by special courtship behavior that helps males and females select one another. For some species, such as right whales, humpbacks, and gray whales, males and females gather at a single location to reproduce, much the way frogs gather in a pond. Once they meet, the competition begins. Some competitions are outright battles, such as those engaged in by narwhals.

HUMPBACK PODS TEND TO BE TIGHTER THAN THOSE OF OTHER BALEEN WHALES.

Humpback mating behavior is even more elaborate. As females gather, they are treated to a full-blown concert from hopeful males. Once the singing ends, the pushing and shoving begins. Male humpbacks are known to charge and slash, head-butt and body-slam one another for quite some time before one male emerges as the female's favorite and principal escort. Even after he earns his favored position, the escort can lose his status while he races around with the female if he isn't on guard.

Sperm whales use a similar mating strategy. Females travel as members of a pod that includes adult females, calves, and both male and female "youngsters." When a female is ready to mate, mature males (nearby in their own group) battle to win her over. After mating occurs, a different male may approach the same female.

FOR BALEEN WHALES, THE RELATIONSHIP BETWEEN A MOTHER AND ITS YOUNG IS A VERY CLOSE ONE DURING THE FIRST YEAR OF LIFE.

Gray whales take a different strategy. Instead of males battling one another directly, they all take a turn mating. The competition to reproduce then takes place inside the female's body, as sperm cells from different males compete to be the one that actually fertilizes the female's egg. Bottlenose dolphin males use a similar mating strategy, as two or three young males may work together to whisk away a female to mate with.

Once mating is complete, the pregnant female usually goes off to the feeding waters while her unborn calf matures inside of her body. A baleen whale's pregnancy typically lasts exactly a year, so the calf is born when the group returns to the breeding waters the following year. The pregnancies of toothed whales, such as the sperm whale, often take more than a year to complete.

6 Whales Up Close

Now let's take a closer look at five different whales—sperm whales, blue whales, humpback whales, killer whales, and gray whales—and what makes them special.

Sperm Whales

At some time each day, after a tough round of diving, the school of about twenty sperm whales surfaces all at once. Normally, the whales would stay up for just ten minutes or so to replenish their oxygen supply. But sometimes these huge creatures take time out to socialize. All at once the whales gather, like enormous ballroom dancers, and glide over one another very slowly, gently touching as they pass each other by.

A visitor to this gathering might be surprised by how gentle and shy sperm whales seem. Are they the fierce killers that Herman Melville portrayed in *Moby Dick*? There is no doubt that sperm whales are powerful animals. They are the largest of the

SPERM WHALES LOVE TO SOCIALIZE.

toothed whales. They have the largest head, the biggest brain, the largest tail fluke, and bigger (and more) teeth, than any other whale. Yet, up close, they don't seem fierce at all. Nearby human and dolphin swimmers seem to upset them, and often cause them to back away.

Perhaps the best way to describe sperm whales is to say that they are divers. They spend most of their day diving, and when they are not diving they are usually recovering from a dive. Generally, a sperm whale dives about once an hour. Almost immediately, unnecessary body functions slow or shut down during a dive. The whale's heart slows. Oxygen moves from the lungs to the muscles. Digestion comes to a stop, and blood flow to some body parts is kept to a minimum.

As the whale slowly descends at a speed of about 3.5 miles per hour (about 6 km/hr), the water gets darker and colder. At a depth of about 825 feet (250 m), the whale switches on its echolocation system and begins to send out clicks at regular intervals, about one per second. Then it listens. It forms a picture of its environment by listening for two reference reflections: the echo from the water surface above, and the echo from the ocean floor below. In between, the whale detects other disturbances, including those made by squid, its primary food source.

When it reaches feeding depth, the whale begins to hunt. Analysis of sperm whale stomachs shows that the whales feed on immense quantities of squid and deep-sea fish. But here lies a major mystery: how can such a big, slow-moving, "ocean liner" of a whale manage to catch up with quick, jet-propelled swimmers like squid? No one knows for sure. Some whale experts think that light from the bioluminescent (glow-in-the-dark) squid reflects off the whale's ghostly white lips, teeth, and mouth to create a glowing "lure" that draws the squid into the whale's mouth.

BUBBLE NETTING REQUIRES THE COOPERATION OF MORE THAN ONE HUMPBACK.

Another theory suggests that sperm whales send out echo-location "shock waves" that stun squid into submission so that they can easily be eaten. Still another idea states that the depths sperm whales dive to are so cold (35 degrees Fahrenheit, or 2 °C), dark, and lacking in oxygen that the whale simply snaps up its sluggish prey, which lies in a sleeplike state of inaction, suspended motionless in the water.

However sperm whales catch their prey, one thing is certain: they do it efficiently. A large sperm whale is likely to consume about 1,100 pounds (500 kg) of squid each day! That's probably about one thousand individual squid—so it seems unlikely that the whale has to chase down each victim, one by one.

Sperm whales are by far the most social of the great whales. Every sperm whale calf is born into a pod—an extended family that includes its mother, cousins, aunts, and grandmothers. In fact, all sperm whales belong to this pod except for older males, who leave at age five or six to join all-male groups. These males will stay in their groups until they are large enough to break off on their own and challenge other mature males to earn the right to mate with female members of a pod.

The battle to approach females has never been witnessed, but the long scars that bull males carry on their heads suggest that they can be fierce. After fighting off rivals, the victorious male is greeted by the pod members as an honored guest. Everyone crowds around the massive champion (adult male sperm whales are much larger than females), cooing and fussing. Even the calves get in on the act: one whale watcher reported witnessing a bull male giving a calf a ride in his flippers.

Pregnancy for sperm whales lasts sixteen months. After

THE GRAY WHALE MOTHER IS VERY GENTLE WITH ITS CALF.

birth, calves are among the most sheltered offspring in the animal world. Everywhere they go they are shielded and protected by the group. Some calves are thought to drink their mother's milk well into their teen years! But built into this lifestyle is a major problem. To feed, all sperm whales must dive. Diving means that mothers abandon their babies for almost an hour at a time. How do the calves stay safe?

In fact, sperm whale experts think that the organization of the pod itself evolved as a sort of "day care" system for calves. While one mother dives, a different mother (aunt, grandmother, older cousin) watches over the calf. When the diving mother returns from below, she may assist in watching over another whale's calf. The result is that each calf is constantly surrounded by at least a few members of the pod, which is usually enough to scare off killer whales, sharks, and other predators.

Identifying Sperm Whales
1. Single blowhole on left side of head, shooting sideways
2. Huge head with distinctive shape
3. Males up to 65 feet (20 m) in length; females smaller
4. Splotchy gray skin; head scratches

Blue Whales

When you see a blue whale, the first and last thing that comes to mind is size. After all, in most cases there seems to be a limit to how big an animal can get. But this creature seems to go way beyond that limit. Its tongue weighs 3 to 4 tons (2,700 to 3,600 kg). Its heart is the size of a car. Some of its blood vessels are big enough for a house cat to crawl through!

What advantage does this great size (up to 110 feet [34 m] in length, 120 tons [109 kg] in weight) give to a blue whale? For

Blue Whale

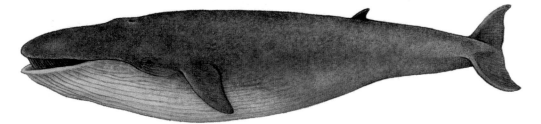

one thing, its large size protects the whale from enemies. What predator would dare attack a creature so large? (In fact, killer whales do attack blue whale calves, but not the adults.) But size has its drawbacks, as well. A large blue whale must eat about 5 tons (9,600 kg) of food each day, just to keep up its weight. That's probably more food than the entire population of your school eats in a week.

Perhaps the ultimate reason why a blue whale is so big is that it *can* be that big. Being supported by water on all sides, weight is not much of a burden to the whale. It moves by pushing against water, not land, so it need not be supported by massive limbs. And the bigger it is, the more the blue whale can eat.

As sleek, swift-swimming rorquals that migrate from breeding to feeding waters each year, blue whales spend only about 120 days of the year eating. But when they eat, they really eat. In fact, all rorquals are like feeding machines that are designed to harvest one of the most abundant food sources on Earth—krill. In the blue whale's polar feeding waters, these shrimplike creatures collect in swarms of unimaginable size. One swarm was estimated to contain 2.5 million tons of krill. That's about 5 billion pounds (2.3 billion kg) of creatures—almost a whole pound for every person on Earth!

Like other rorquals, blue whales gulp rather than skim their food. This typically requires a whale to size up a good swarm of krill, swoop down under it, and with its mouth banked at a 30-degree angle, take in up to 60 tons (54,000 kg) of prey-filled water. This is done repeatedly and tirelessly during the feeding season, and turns out to be a rather solitary task. While blue whales are sometimes seen in pairs and small groups, their lives appear be rather lonely, like other rorquals. Perhaps because they need to trawl over a large area, blues tend to spread out and travel by themselves, avoiding the chattering social lives of sperm whales, orcas, and other toothed whales.

However, the life of a blue may not be as lonely as it seems. As humans, we tend to associate closeness with actual physical distance. But who is to say that blue whales don't use sound to bridge long distances and keep in touch? In fact, blue whales routinely issue a stream of ultra low frequency, ultra loud (180 decibels) sounds that can be heard for miles around. Scientists have detected some of these sounds at distances of up to 1,500 miles (2,400 km) or more. Are these amazingly loud sounds a form of communication that keeps whales close over long distances? At this point, scientists are not sure.

Identifying Blue Whales

1. Huge size
2. Sleek rorqual shape
3. U-shaped head when seen from above (fin whale is similar, but its head is V-shaped)
4. Dark gray blue with mottled back and sides
5. Fast swimming: at least 19 miles per hour (30 km/hr)
6. Spout appears single even though it comes from double blowhole; up to 30 feet (9 m) in height straight up

Humpback Whales

If there were a popularity contest for whales, the humpbacks would probably win it. Though large and powerful (females reach lengths of 62 feet, or 19 meters) humpbacks are natural performers. They often make a series of spectacular leaps and dives, seemingly just for the fun of it. At the same time, humpbacks not only show little fear of people, but they actually seem interested in them. They often approach boats to get a closer look at their occupants. In the nineteenth century, this trusting nature made humpbacks an easy target for whalers. But in today's world, these acrobatic giants are a solid favorite among whale watchers the world over.

What makes humpbacks such crowd pleasers? Probably not their outward appearance. Though humpbacks are part of the sleek rorqual whale family, they are more squat (and less sleek) than other rorquals. They have giant flippers (the biggest of any whale), odd tubercles on their heads that look like stiff cat whiskers, and unsightly callosities that are covered with whale lice (amphipods) and barnacles.

In many ways, humpbacks behave like typical rorqual whales. They are seasonal creatures, migrating long distances to their summer feeding waters in the Arctic and returning to warmer breeding waters in winter. But humpbacks also show some surprising behaviors that are not shared by other rorqual, or baleen, whales.

When feeding, most rorquals simply scoop up krill and other small creatures in large gulps, plowing ahead like tractors in a field. Humpbacks go far beyond this, perfecting a variety of clever feeding techniques that include lunge feeding, flick feeding, kick feeding, and bubble feeding. Lunge feeding involves making the same driving head thrust that fin whales make, but

EACH WHALE HAS DISTINCTIVE MARKINGS ON ITS FLUKE.

a humpback finishes off the lunge with a sharp slap of its huge flipper, herding the small fish and krill into its gaping mouth. Flick feeding uses the tail fluke to push a wave of small animals mouthward. Kick feeding is similar to flick feeding, except the fluke smacks its prey forward rather than push the water ahead on a wave.

The most remarkable feeding technique that humpbacks use is bubble feeding. Here, a whale creates a column of bubbles to herd prey into a tight formation for easy capture. Surprisingly, different humpback populations use different bubble feeding methods. Humpbacks of the North Atlantic often just send out huge ball-shaped clouds of bubbles to herd prey. Pacific whales never make bubble clouds. Instead they swim in a swirling spiral to create a cylinder-shaped bubble net.

The other amazing trait that distinguishes humpbacks from other rorquals (and all other whales) is their singing. Sailors on eighteenth- and nineteenth-century whaling ships were puzzled by the haunting moans they heard in the night. These sounds were once thought to have supernatural origin. When pioneering whale researcher Roger Payne identified them as humpback songs and recorded them as the best-selling collection, *Songs of the Humpback Whale*, a new question arose: are humpback songs real songs that are genuinely musical? In fact, research by Payne and others has shown that humpback songs clearly qualify as music. They have a beginning, an end, a theme, and repeatable musical phrases that resemble melodies in human music. If a whale needs to interrupt a song—to go to the surface to breathe, for example—when he returns to the water he continues the song exactly where he left off!

So while it appears that humpback songs are genuinely musical, the question now becomes, what is the purpose of these songs? Most evidence points to the idea that humpback songs are "love songs." For one thing, only males sing the songs, and they are almost always sung during the breeding season. It is likely that females use the songs, which vary in different humpback populations, to select males for mating.

Identifying Humpback Whales
1. Extremely large flippers
2. Rorqual shape but less sleek than other rorquals
3. A great performer of breaches, splashes, rolls, and leaps
4. Skin covered with barnacles and growths
5. Females up to 62 feet (19 m) in length
6. Spout is wide, V-shaped, and highly visible against the sky

Orcas—Killer Whales

To many animals that live in or near the water, a glimpse of long, delta-shaped dorsal fins can mean only one thing: killer whales.

While measuring only 30 feet (9 m) or so in length, the killer whale, or orca, is classified as a large dolphin. Unlike its tame relatives, the killer whale is recognized as one of the most feared predators on land or sea. In many respects, killer whales are the wolves of the oceans. They hunt in packs and are often able to out-swim, outsmart, wait out, or overpower a wide variety of prey. The killer whale is the only whale that preys on other whale species, including the calves of some of the largest whales. Surprisingly, killer whales in captivity have proven to be friendly, intelligent, and gentle.

Like the sperm whale, killer whales are highly social animals that live in close-knit family pods of about ten individuals. However, orca pods differ from sperm whale pods in one important respect: they include both male and female adults. Also, male and female killer whales often stay in the same pod for life.

Within the pod, killer whales lead a wide-ranging life in which they hunt, play, and explore together. The pod itself is a remarkably fluid association that forms and re-forms in many different arrangements. Like social groups of people, killer whales have their own extended family. They also have special friends within the family with whom they spend time participating in specialized activities.

Each pod is also remarkable because it has its own customs and traditions that differ from those of other pods. For example, killer whale communication includes a dialect of clicks, whistles, and squawks that is unique to each pod. In British Columbia, each of twenty different orca pods has its own vocabulary. Human researchers can distinguish, for example, J-Pod from K-Pod (each pod is named for a letter of the alphabet) just by listening to the sounds that each pod makes. Pods in other parts of the world have their own unique dialects as well.

Killer whale customs even extend to hunting and recreation

time. For example, the killer whales of British Columbia often spend their leisure time off Vancouver Island massaging themselves by swimming rapidly against the pebble-covered bottom, while killer whales of the Crozet Islands in the Indian Ocean swim slowly through dense kelp beds for their massages.

Hunting strategies for killer whales are as varied as the whales themselves. The killer whale diet includes fish, sea birds, seals and other sea mammals, and squid. The most remarkable hunting feats of killer whales probably involve hunting seals on beaches. This is done using a variety of strategies. Crozet Island killer whales come to a special beach during the elephant seal breeding season. Instead of attacking right away, the orcas stay in the shallow water and wait. While waiting, sometimes for weeks, mother orcas teach their young to hunt. Finally, the killer whales pounce, lurching onto dry land to snatch a seal pup. It is a remarkably bold and dangerous maneuver, as the whales run the risk of going too far and getting stranded on the beach.

In Argentina, even more elaborate seal-hunting strategies are used. There, pod mates may hunt in pairs, with one whale making a grab for a seal, while its partner waits a few feet in the water, looking to scoop up nearby pups that panic and flee during its partner's attack.

Identifying Killer Whales

1. White eye patch, black back, gray saddle patch
2. Distinctive vertical dorsal fin
3. Sleek smooth skin
4. Males up to 30 feet (9 m) in length
5. Very social and friendly; will approach boats and hop, leap, breach, and play

Gray Whales

Once known as "devil fish" for their ferocious ability to fight against capture, gray whales are slow-moving, skim-feeding, baleen whales. At one point they were thought to live in both the North Atlantic and the Pacific, but now gray whales are found only in the Pacific. They are perhaps the most reliable migrators of any whale species. Their regular appearance at various locations along the west coast of North America has made gray whales star performers at many whale-watching locations.

At one point, the fate of gray whales was very much in question. Since they frequent shallow coastal waters, grays were always quite easy to find and kill. In his 1874 book, *The Marine Mammals of the Northwest Coast of North America*, author Charles Scammon writes of discovering gray whale breeding lagoons in Baja, California, in which dozens of pregnant females would gather in extremely shallow water, "resting heavily on the sandy bottom, until the rising tide floated them." Here, the whalers were able to slaughter gray whales by the hundred. It is thought that grays might have become extinct had not the demand for whale products dropped after the discovery of underground petroleum oil in Pennsylvania in 1859.

However easy they were to find, gray whales did not submit to capture easily. Scammon writes of a single devil fish in 1856 that destroyed two whaling boats, damaged several others, and injured six of the eighteen sailors, two of them severely.

Gray whales are extremely slow swimmers that eat primarily by bottom feeding in shallow coastal waters. They gouge out huge ruts in the ocean bottom wherever they feed, filtering out tiny shrimplike amphipods, which are similar to the krill that most rorqual whales eat.

A ban on gray whale hunting was enacted in 1946. Despite being slow breeders, gray whales have re-established themselves nicely and appear to be a great comeback story, now reaching a population of 20,000 or more. As long as they are not being attacked by harpoons, these creatures are gentle and friendly, often sidling up to boats to be stroked and petted.

Identifying Gray Whales

1. Females up to 50 feet (15 m) in length; males smaller
2. Low, V-shaped, or heart-shaped plume
3. Adults covered with whale lice (amphipods) and barnacles
4. Has thicker baleen than rorqual whales
5. Slow swimming, but often breaches, and hops
6. Young whales in particular are friendly and will approach boats

GRAY WHALES ARE AS CURIOUS ABOUT PEOPLE AS PEOPLE ARE ABOUT THEM.

7 Looking Ahead

Something about whales touches a special place in the human imagination. Whale watchers often tell the same story to describe their first encounter with a whale: it was so much bigger than they thought—so calm and gentle, so noble.

Is it wrong to value cetaceans over other animal species, especially other endangered species? Are whales more important, more worth saving, than say, bison, butterflies, or Bengal tigers? More importantly, do we really need to worry about saving whales anymore, now that the International Whaling Commission's (IWC's)1986 complete ban on whaling has been in effect for more than fifteen years? For that matter, what does it mean to "save" whales? Does it mean that no whale should be killed or endangered in any way, under any circumstances whatsoever? Does it mean that we won't be satisfied until all whale populations are restored to their pre-whaling levels? Or are we satisfied if whale populations just continue to grow, even if they now represent less than 10 percent of their original numbers?

ARE THE CLAIMS OF FISHING COMPANIES THAT THEIR NETS ARE "DOLPHIN FRIENDLY" REALLY TRUE?

All of these questions are difficult if not impossible to answer in any absolute way. The story of whales and people is complicated. In many early cultures, whales and whalers had a special bond, and a great deal of respect for one another. Many indigenous whalers, such as the Inuit from Alaska, held special rituals for the whales they killed, thanking them, praying for them, and apologizing to them for needing to take their lives.

But respect soon gave way to greed. By 1850, the height of the whaling era, hundreds of whaling ships spanned the globe in search of their prize. Whaling started with right whales—the "right whale to kill"—which were soon replaced by bowhead, gray whales, and sperm whales. When each species became scarce, the whalers just moved on to a new kind of whale, or a new territory. The only whales that seemed to be off-limits to everyone were the speedy rorquals. In 1851, Herman Melville wrote that "There is no means known to catch a fin whale or its fast cousins." Yet, within twenty years, new steam-powered whaling ships and explosive harpoons made even the rorquals vulnerable.

The slaughter didn't stop until well into the twentieth century, after millions of whales were killed. By 1986, when all whaling was supposed to have ended, many whale populations stood at only a fraction of their size before the whaling era began in the seventeenth century.

In the aftermath of this great slaughter, many of us look back and wonder how this could have happened. What we forget, of course, was that whaling used to be big business. In the 1840s, joining a whaling ship was thought to be a great opportunity to get ahead for those without land, a trade, or personal fortune. (However, some volunteers quickly became disillusioned. As one not-so-happy nineteenth century whaling-voyage veteran said, "Any man who . . . has a log hut . . . and would consent to leave . . . on a whale voyage is a proper subject for a lunatic asylum.")

A PURSE-SEINE TUNA FISHING NET ENCIRCLES THE FISH AND IS THEN SLOWLY DRAWN IN, OFTEN TRAPPING DOLPHINS. TO SAVE THE DOLPHINS, THE NETS ARE EQUIPPED WITH ESCAPE HATCHES.

Only after the long years of killing did the world slowly decide whales should be saved. The first hunting ban in the world was put into place in 1931 (1935 in the United States) to protect bowhead. We would like to think the ban was a product of high-minded thinking. In fact, it occurred because so few whales were left. Bowhead had been hunted nearly to extinction. If whalers didn't stop, there would have been no bowhead whales left to kill at all.

In 1935, a ban was put on right whale hunting. Then bans were established on the hunting of grays, humpbacks, blues, seis, and, in 1984, sperm whales. In 1986 the IWC put a stop to all whaling. Still, hunting continued. Norway refused to sign the ban treaty. Japan continued to whale for what they claimed to be scientific research purposes. Many indigenous groups, such as the

Makah Indians in Washington state, killed whales for traditional purposes. And Russian whaling ships simply ignored the ban and kept on killing whales in secret for many years.

Other Dangers

Thanks to the efforts of anti-whaling groups, whaling has slowed to a trickle in the twenty-first century. While no cetaceans have become extinct in the past one hundred years, many have come close, including those that are currently most endangered: the northern right whale, which numbers about 320, and almost every variety of river dolphin, including the baiji from China, the vaquita of Mexico, and the river dolphins of India and Pakistan.

But just as hunting pressures have decreased, new threats to cetaceans have emerged. The most serious of these include fishing, water pollution, habitat loss, collisions, and noise pollution. Fishing mainly affects dolphin populations—giant nets used by modern fishing boats are especially dangerous to these species. While the fishing industry doesn't seek to kill dolphins, they often get tangled in fishing nets and are difficult to set free without destroying expensive equipment.

Protests from conservation groups have created "dolphin friendly" net systems that use escape doors and human observers to help free trapped cetaceans. But there is no telling how effective, or how widespread, these measures really are.

More troublesome to the future of cetaceans is pollution in various forms. Sources of pollution include untreated sewage, oil spills, industrial and agricultural wastes, and chemicals that are dumped into the ocean. The effects of pollution are often difficult to measure. Poisons that kill instantly are easy to monitor, but substances that cause disease, health problems, and birth defects often act over long periods of time. Their effects are difficult to measure or evaluate. Many chemicals collect in plankton, which are then eaten by small fish, which themselves are eaten by squid and larger fish. By the time whales eat these larger creatures at the top of the food chain, the toxic chemicals are collected in a much more concentrated form. While it is impossible to assign blame to any single source of pollution, over time the prolonged exposure takes its toll. This is seen most clearly in river dolphins, whose habitats are being both polluted and destroyed as developers continue to turn fragile river ecosystems into recreational and residential zones.

THIS GRAY WHALE CALF HAS BEEN IN CAPTIVITY AND IS ABOUT TO RELEASED BACK INTO THE WILD.

More Special than Others?

Many questions about whales are based on the assumption that these huge creatures are more intelligent and sensitive than other animals. Indeed, some whale supporters talk of whales as "spiritual beings" that live on a plane as high or higher than that of human beings. Is there any truth to these claims?

There is no doubt that whales are intelligent creatures. The sperm whale has the largest brain of any animal on Earth. Dolphins have brains that are about 6 percent larger than humans. But does a big brain mean that an animal is intelligent? Researchers point out that there is absolutely no evidence of a connection between brain size and intelligence in humans, so why should there be one for whales?

On the other hand, brain size in proportion to body size does

NOT ALL POLLUTION IS AS VISIBLE AS THIS.

seem to have some connection to intelligence. Of all mammals, humans have the largest brain-to-body ratio. Whales come in second on this list. Whales also show signs of intelligence in their behavior. Examples of cetacean intelligence include: humpbacks working together in clever ways to create bubble nets; killer whales developing ingenious methods for capturing seals on beaches; and sperm whales showing amazingly sensitive and cooperative group behavior. Many toothed whales, including killer whales and sperm whales, show a sophisticated use of sound that in many ways resembles language. Other whales, such as humpbacks and bowheads, sing amazingly complex songs.

People who work with whales attribute all sorts of human qualities to them. Roger Payne, for example, tells of male southern right whales acting "suave" or turning on their "charm" as they approached a group of females. Trainers for dolphin shows tell of the great ease with which cetaceans catch on to stunts and tricks. More troubling are tragic reports of whale strandings, especially among pilot whales, in which a single whale, or a group of more than a dozen whales are left to die on the beach all at once. Theories to explain these mysterious strandings include navigational errors due to magnetic disturbances, response to noise pollution, and disease. Some researchers feel that strandings are a form of mass suicide that a group commits when one of its members goes astray. They see this as a sign of great sympathy and intelligence.

On the other hand, people who work with other animals describe equally impressive achievements. Birds and frogs sing complex songs. Dog owners tell of animals that can anticipate their every move. Researchers have shown that chimpanzees can learn and even teach each other a kind of language. Are these feats of intelligence equal to, or greater than, the evidence for intelligent cetaceans? No one knows for sure. In fact, while cetaceans are clearly very intelligent creatures, the idea that they are more "special"—and therefore more deserving of being saved—than other animals remains an open question.

The Future

Few animals have been hunted down over the centuries as relentlessly as the great whales. Today, more than fifteen years after the 1986 whaling ban, Japan and some other countries (and groups) are still hunting whales. But for the most part, killing whales on a large-scale basis has stopped. The question now becomes, will whale populations ever return to their original, pre-whaling sizes?

Some whale populations, such as the California gray whales, have done remarkably well. The northern right whale, on the other hand, has been protected for more than 65 years and still has a population of only a few hundred.

Most whale populations are slowly increasing. As large mammals that reproduce slowly, one calf at a time, you might expect the replenishment process to take many years. On the other hand, some whale experts doubt that whales will ever reach their former population levels. They think that whales have lost their niche in the ocean food chain and have been replaced by other krill eaters, such as penguins and seals.

Are these experts correct? Without accurate population figures it is hard to tell whether the situation is actually getting better or worse. Population data is critical for making decisions about whales, but obtaining reliable data is tricky. How do you get a good measure of the population of animals that spend most of their lives unseen, underwater, and often hundreds or even thousands of miles away from human population centers? It's difficult, but scientists are developing new ways to identify whales

To keep track of whales, scientists attach electronic transmitters to them.

using such tools as tail fluke photographs, radio transmitters, DNA analysis, and underwater microphones.

Once accurate population figures are made, then people can start making decisions about whether the whales are being "saved" or not. For example, it may turn out that the hidden dangers of such things as pollution, fishing, and habitat destruction are causing more problems than would be expected. One possible danger for whales is noise pollution. Recently, mass strandings have been noticed in places near large military sonar installations. Were underwater sonar signals confusing whales or damaging their ears, causing them to veer off course into danger? Scientists are still collecting data to try to solve this problem. If sonar does harm whales, they suspect that other underwater noise pollution—such as drilling and shipping noise—may be harming whales as well.

People may disagree about things in the environment that harm whales, but some whales are still in grave danger. Some steps to be taken seem clear. First, while no whale has become extinct in the past century, a few cetacean species are close to extinction. Measures should be taken to preserve and protect these creatures (baijis and northern right whales, for example).

Second, needless killing of cetaceans should be stopped, or at least kept to an absolute minimum. The situation for tuna fishing is a tricky one. How can dolphins be protected without causing great harm to the tuna fishing industry? It also appears that northern right whales are being killed by passing ships as they sleep near the surface of the water. Finally, noise pollution may be harming whales in untold ways, causing strandings and interrupting natural migration and breeding patterns. More research into these questions may shed some light on courses of action to take to help preserve these whales.

Third, steps should be taken to curb pollution on a global basis—not just to help whales, but to preserve the diversity of all life forms, including humans. For too long, people have treated their local environments as dumping grounds for wastes, chemicals, and byproducts of industrial processes. The effects of these thoughtless acts have so far been more directly felt on land, and especially in fresh water lakes and rivers. The resilience of the oceans is almost entirely based on their vast size: the amount of ocean water is several million times the total volume of fresh water on the planet. But this does not mean the oceans are unaffected by pollution. Indeed, many shallow whale-breeding waters may be threatened by habitat destruction even now. Perhaps the world should begin looking at the environmental, as well as economic, costs of the goods they make and the actions they take. Prices should reflect not only the cost of producing and marketing a product, but also how much it will cost to clean up the mess that making the product created.

Fourth, everyone can agree that the comeback of gray

whales, humpbacks, and blue whales is a good sign. Other whale populations are also steadily increasing to the point where whaling countries will ask to resume whaling. This is another tricky question. Are whale species, if they are no longer endangered, entitled to be protected any more than say, bison or African elephants?

HUMAN EFFORTS TO SAVE WHALES THAT ARE STRANDED OR STUCK UNDER THE ICE ARE SOMETIMES, BUT NOT ALWAYS, SUCCESSFUL.

SCIENTISTS COLLECT DATA TO SEE IF WHALE POPULATIONS ARE INCREASING OR DECREASING.

Perhaps the answer to this question lies in how whales are ultimately regarded by humans. Are whales now considered more than mere creatures or animals that we feel entitled to use for our own selfish purposes? This question is open to debate. What is perhaps more certain is that cetaceans are not only magnificent creatures, but they are also mirrors that we can hold up to our own sense of self-respect and justice. Is a world in which whales are treasured, protected, and respected a better place to live than a world in which whales are hunted or thoughtlessly harmed? The answer seems obvious, yet in which world we ultimately choose to live is something that only the future can reveal.

Glossary

adaptation—a change in body form or function as a result of natural selection

ambergris—an oily substance from a sperm whale's digestive tract that is used to make perfume, and is very rare and valuable

baleen—springy, hornlike filter that whales use to catch food; also called a whalebone.

bends—decompression sickness that occurs when a diver surfaces and nitrogen gas comes out of solution in the blood

blowhole—a breathing hole on the top of a whale's head; baleen whales have double blowholes and toothed whales have a single blowhole

blubber—body fat

breach—a jump of a whale out of the water

bubble nets—columns of bubbles that humpback whales make to catch fish

callosities—misshapen growths that form on the heads of some whales

cetacean—any member of the whale family

density—how heavy something is per unit volume; for example, iron has greater density than aluminum

displacement—the amount of liquid, such as water, that is moved aside when an object is placed in the liquid

DNA—deoxyribonucleic acid—the substance inside every cell that contains the genetic code; DNA is used to determine the relationship among different animal species

echolocation—a sensory system that uses sound echoes to "see" the environment

ectotherm—cold-blooded animal that mainly relies on its environment for heat

endotherm—warm-blooded animal that generates its own body heat

fluke—horizontal tail of a whale

habitat—the environment in which an animal species lives

harpoon—a spearlike weapon that was used to hunt whales

krill—shrimplike creature that many baleen whales eat (*euphausiids*)

lob-tail—smacking the water with the tail fluke; similar to breaching

mammals—animals that have hair and give milk; whales and human beings are mammals

melon—-spongy, liquid-filled area of a sperm whale's head that is thought to control diving depth

migration—the act of traveling a great distance to reach a breeding or feeding location during a particular season in the year

mysticetes—baleen, or toothless, whales

natural selection—the process of selecting traits that increase the chances of an animal's survival

ondontocetes—toothed whales

oxygen—chemical gas that all animals use to burn their food to get energy

plankton—any ocean life form that drifts rather than swims actively

pod—social group of whales

population—the number of whales in any given species

pressure—force created by the liquid or gas surrounding a solid object

rorquals—sleek baleen whale family that includes the blue, fin, and humpback whales

species—group of related organisms capable of interbreeding and producing fertile offspring

spermaceti—very high quality oil that comes from a sperm whale

spout—exhaled air (not water) from a whale's blowhole; different types of whales have characteristic spout shapes

stranding—when one or more whales die on a beach

Species Checklist

The list below identifies the whale species living in the world today. Like all living things, whales are given both common and scientific names. Common names are usually written in lowercase, unless taken from a proper name. Scientific names, which are in Latin, should be italicized with the first, or generic, name capitalized and the second, which identifies the species, in lowercase.

baiji *Lipotes vexillifer*
Beluga *Delphinapterus leucas*
blue whale *Balaenoptera musculus*
bottlenose dolphin *Tursiops truncatus*
bowhead whale *Balaena mysticetus*
Bryde's whale *Balaenoptera edeni*
fin whale *Balaenoptera physalus*
gray whale *Eschrichtius robustus*
humpback whale *Megaptera novaeangliae*
killer whale *Orcinus orca*
minke whale *Balaenoptera acutorostrata*
narwhal *Monodon monoceros*
northern bottlenose whale *Hyperoodon ampullatus*
northern right whale *Eubalaena glacialis*
pilot whale *Globicephala melaena*
sei whale *Balaenoptera borealis*
southern right whale *Eubalaena australis*
sperm whale *Physeter macrocephalus*
Vaquita *Phocoena sinus*

These species aren't specifically mentioned in the text:

Baird's beaked whale *Berardius bairdii*
Cuvier's beaked whale *Ziphius cavirostris*
common dolphin *Delphinus delphis*
Dall's porpoise *Phocoenoides dalli*
spectacled porpoise *Australophocaena dioptrica*

Further Research

Here are some recommended resources for further research on whales.

Books for Young People

Carwardine, Mark. *Whales, Dolphins, & Porpoises*. New York: Dorling Kindersley, 1995.

Carwardine, Mark, Erich Hoyt, R. Ewan Fordyce, and Peter Gill. *Whales, Dolphins, & Porpoises*. New York: Time-Life Books, 1998.

Gordon, Jonathan. *Sperm Whales*. Stillwater, MN: Voyageur Press, 1998.

Papastavrou, Vassili. *Whale*. New York: Knopf, 1993.

Videos

In the Company of Whales–Gentle Giants of the Watery Realm. Discovery Channel Communications, Inc., 1992.
Whale Watch. Nova, 1994.
Killer Whales: Wolves of the Sea. National Geographic, 1993.

Museum

New Bedford Whaling Museum, Cold Spring Harbor, New York.

Web Sites

American Cetacean Society
http://www.acsonline.org

World Wildlife Fund
http://www.worldwildlife.org

New Bedford Whaling National Park
http://www.onps.gov/nebe

WhaleNet
http://whale.wheelock.edu/Welcome.html

The Cetacean Society International
http://csiwhalesalive.org

Bibliography

These are the resources that were most useful in researching this book. Although the publications listed here may include some information that is a bit technical for young readers, they are all worthwhile for those with a strong interest in whales.

Books and Articles

Bonner, Nigel. *Whales of the World*. New York: Facts on File, 1993.

Clapham, Phil. *Whales of the World*. Stillwater, MN: Voyageur Press, 1997.

Ellis, Richard. *The Book of Whales*. New York: Knopf, 1988.

Gray, Patricia M., Bernie Krause, Jelle Atema, Roger Payne, Carol Krumhansl, and Luis Baptista, Biology and Music: "Enhanced: The Music of Nature and the Nature of Music," *Science* 291, 5501, 2000.

Klinowska, Margaret, "Brain, Behavior, and Intelligence in Cetaceans," *High North Publication 11*, September 26, 1994.

Index